PLUM BRANDY

PLUM BRANDY

CROATIAN JOURNEYS

JOSIP NOVAKOVICH

WHITE PINE PRESS • BUFFALO, NEW YORK

Acknowledgments: Thanks to the editors of the publications in which these essays appeared: "Grandmother's Tongue," *Kenyon Review*; "A Meditation on Wood," *Poet Lore*; "Deceptive Pleasures of Chess," *Ruminator Review*; "Sawdust Memories," *Witness*; "Daily Bread," *Poet Lore*; "A Homecoming," *Boulevard*; "An Anti-Story," *Iowa Review*, *Minneapolis Star Tribune* & *Cleveland Plain Dealer*; "Croatian Travelogue," *Boulevard*; "Countries Without Bridges," *New Letters*; "A Place in Between," *New Letters*; "Hvar," *New York Times* Travel Section; "Thin and Fat Cats," *Ruminator Review*; "Letter From Croatia," *Michigan Quarterly Review*; "A Train Romance," *Witness*; "On Finding a Grave in Cleveland," *Prairie Schooner*.

"Countries Without Bridges" won a Pushcart Prize honorable mention. "A Place In Between" was listed as a Distinguished Essay in *Best American Essays 1998*. "Sawdust Memories" was listed as a Distinguished Essay in *Best American Essays 2001*. "Secret Spaces of Childhood" appeared in the anthology *Secrecy* published by Graywolf Press in 2000. "My Son's Views" appeared in *110 Stories*, an anthology published by New York University Press in 2002.

The author thanks the National Endowment for the Arts and the Guggenheim Foundation for their support; the New York Public Library's Dorothy and Lewis B. Cullman Center for Scholars and Writers; Richard Burgin, Peter Stine, and Robert Stewart for their encouragement; and Elaine LaMattina for insightfully editing and designing the book.

Publication of this book was made possible, in part, by grants from
the National Endowment for the Arts and with public funds from the
New York State Council on the Arts, a State Agency.

Cover photograph copyright ©2003 Jon Hughes.

Printed and bound in the United States of America.

Library of Congress Control Number: 2003100355

First Edition

Published by
White Pine Press
P.O. Box 236
Buffalo, New York 14201
www.whitepine.org

For Eva and Joseph

CONTENTS

INTRODUCTION

ON THE ART
OF VISITING YOUR HOMELAND

It's amazing how a country changes through time. I have had the privilege, though living away from the former Yugoslavia, to visit in intervals of two years, so I could see the drastic shifts from one Yugoslavia to another—or rather, to many—and one Croatia to another, one Bosnia to another. "You can't step in the same river twice" can be paraphrased as "You can't enter the same country twice," in the Balkans. Well, the famous saying of Heraclitus— "Nothing endures but change."—comes from the Balkans anyway. At first, it was the entering part, and even more the exiting, that gave me anxiety attacks. I grew up with the mythology of border terror; and since I emigrated at the age of twenty as a potential draftee, I actually had good reason to fear being snatched down from a train. Some of my visits I described in my previous collection of essays, which I titled *Apricots from Chernobyl*, using a travelogue set in Russia and Ukraine as the title piece simply because it sounded paradoxical as a metaphor for Communism's juicy promises and toxic deliveries. Anyway, the war was going on in Croatia and the former Yugoslavia, but hardly anybody knew the book had much to do with that topic. At my readings, elderly Ukranians would show up, and they would feel cheated when realizing that I had little to say about Ukraine.

Here, I present travel stories, memoirs, reflections, and character portraits mostly from *1993* until *2002*, but I also give glimpses of the former Yugoslavia as I remember it from the seventies and eighties, with bits of the ghost of my father, who died when I was eleven, my friends, acquaintances, and strangers. But I won't say this is autobiographical or biographical writing, but rather topographical, with the place and its atmosphere dominating the stories. I may detour, but the thoughts come back to Croatia, as do I. So here you have views of an expatriate who occasionally is tempted to become an ex-expatriate, to return home. The problem is, home has changed. I am perfectly happy to be an American in search of a lost place and time through multiple views and perspectives and visits. I could have instead traveled all over the world and become totally global, but I find fascination in redoing the same trip, which turns out to be always thoroughly new and different in more astonishing ways than any exotically new and far-flung place could be.

PROLOGUE

TAKO JE TO

I don't have enough breath to tell this smoothly. I don't know where my drawing of breath should take place and where the lines should be breathless and broken. Never mind: this unsyncopated verselessness does not seek artfulness of expression but is as simple a lament as possible.

Well, in Cleveland there is a man who came here some fifty years ago. He had worked since his early teens as a grocery store assistant in a Jewish merchant's store in Sarajevo. The war came. Djeba's boss hid from the Nazis, and Djeba was drafted at gunpoint into the quisling Bosnian army. The army was defeated, and it surrendered to the British in Slovenia under the promise of some kind of amnesty. The British passed the POWs on to Tito's partisans, who strafed the company, which huddled together. The POWs didn't even have a place to fall on the ground, and many corpses remained standing. Djeba, unhit, curled down below the mess of bleeding corpses, inhaling urine and blood.

When you are hanged, you have an erection. When you are struck down, or before it, you piss. And then bleed. The standing corpses fell like dominos, piling up in two to three levels. At the bottom, Djeba didn't dare move from under the mound of corpses for hours, but when he nearly suffocated, he crawled from under the foul flesh.

Hiding, he chose the most difficult mountains to go back to Bosnia, where he lived in the woods and in a cave for two years, in fear that the partisans might still execute him. He ate tree roots, wild onions, berries, frogs. Driven by hunger in the winter, he walked over the same mountain ridges through Slovenia to Austria and reached a refugee camp. He looked for his former boss from Sarajevo in Vienna and found him. The former boss, a survivor of harrows himself, took his former grocery boy under his wing. Djeba worked in the survivor's new grocery store. Got a visa to the States. Worked for the Tack and Screw Company in Cleveland, living on bread and water.

He saved enough money to buy books. He opened a bookstore, the only Croatian bookstore on the North American continent, on St. Clair and 62nd. Yugoslav secret agents demolished his store several times and threatened to kill him. He repaired the store and kept selling books in Croatian so the words would not die out, so the people would not die out.

The first time I came to the States, my Slovene grandmother took me to the store, in 1974, and there I met the man and his books. She bought me a large dictionary in red covers. My grandmother, who was a partisan nurse in Croatia and Slovenia in the war, died. She is buried in the Calvary cemetery with her bachelor brother, who joined her in Cleveland so they could die together. That may not have been the plan, but they died two weeks apart and ended up in a singular grave.

I have visited Cleveland many times, and each time I stop by this bookstore. The Croatian, Slovenian, and Hungarian neighborhood on the East Side fell apart. It became inner-city black. Out of racism or fear, many whites fled to the suburbs. Slovenes and Croats were the last to follow, perhaps not because of the lack of phobia and racism but because of poverty, and there are still many of them in that neighborhood, including the bookstore man, Djeba.

He does not hate, he does not fear, he sells books. His brother

He showed me how he grows his flower garden. He waters the red flowers lovingly. He showed me how he eats. A bit of bread with olive oil and half an onion and several lettuce leaves. He was eighty-five. We could not talk much. He was nearly deaf. His eyes, cataract ringed, looked steadily, and he nodded often. *Tako je to*, he kept saying. *That is how it is.*

After my visit, a young man robbed him. Knocked him down on the floor. Kicked him and broke his ribs. Smashed his face. Took his wallet. The man who got up from under the mound of foul corpses in the last world war didn't get up. Was found by his friend, a librarian. Taken to the hospital. He recovered in a month and went back to the bookstore. He still runs it. He is not moving to suburbia. He loves his neighborhood, his books, his language. Do I love books that much? Who does?

And there he is, exposed, old, deaf, nearly blind, with his books of beautiful islands and ugly histories. Anybody can walk in and knock him down. But so far he is still standing. Next time I go to Cleveland, I will buy one old, yellowing novel and a jar of red *ajvar*: red tomatoes mixed with red peppers. We will sit down and drink mineral water from Croatia, and he will say, *Tako je to.*

SAWDUST
MEMORIES

GRANDMOTHER'S TONGUE

As a kid in Croatia I learned that I had an American grand-mother through eavesdropping on my parents during tax time, when my father, a clogmaker—that is, a "private entrepreneur," a residue of capitalism to be gotten rid of in socialism—feared that he would be thrown into jail for lack of money.

"Why don't you write to your mother?" Father said. "She could get us out of this crap."

"No, she couldn't. She's old and can barely take care of herself."

"Nonsense, she's an American."

"So?"

"Write to her. She could send us papers, and we could move there."

"Yeah, right, like they need wooden shoes over there."

"I've had it with your pessimism. When I married you, I thought you were some kind of American; that means optimism. We'd man-age there; let's just get the hell out of here."

"Is that why you married me?"

"Come on!"

They talked in Croatian, but I remember it in English. I've for-gotten the sound of my father's voice in Croatian; he died when I was eleven. He had often dreamed of America. I remember how he and I stared at a postcard of Lincoln Center's golden Atlases holding up the gilded, hollow globe. A Baptist minister had mailed it to him.

If it weren't for my grandfather Pavle's poverty at the turn of the century, Mary would not have become my grandmother, and I would not exist, so no matter how absurd the meeting between Pavle and Mary appears to be, I must respect it as the source of my life. Pavle emigrated from Austria-Hungary; in that pre-photograph passport era, he managed to use an Austrian cow's export certificate to get into the States. He spoke no English, so when looking for the address of an acquaintance who would help him settle, the bus driver stopped in front of the address and found it easier to pull Pavle to the house than to speak to him. Pavle advanced in his job at a screw factory, and on the day when he was promoted to a managerial position, at the age of twenty-eight, he felt self-confident. He walked by a yard where he saw a pretty girl of fifteen. He went to the house, rang the bell, introduced himself to the girl's father, told him where he worked and how much he made, and asked whether he could marry the girl. The father said yes. They married the following weekend; it's not clear whether Mary had any say over this. This was before World War I. Mary gave birth to my mother, and they lived in Cleveland until she was three, when Pavle, a Greek-Catholic Croat, heard that a wonderful new country was formed: Kingdom of Serbs, Croats, and Slovenes, small nations which were hitherto victims of empires. Together the South Slavs would be strong. He sold everything he had and moved his family to what would soon be renamed Yugoslavia. He did not want to live in a city, so he bought a piece of land in the hills near the Sava River in Medjuric, not far from Kutina, and tilled the stingy soil for the rest of his days as, to my mind, one of the first American hippies.

He was a poor peasant, barely subsisting in an old wooden house next to that of his older brother, who often stole Pavle's wheat and chickens. Pavle's high taxes mostly went to the Serb king in Belgrade. Pavle believed in Yugoslavia nevertheless, unlike his wife, who hated the village mud and listened to the shortwave radio, pining for America.

Pavle got offers to work in Zagreb as a clerk and interpreter but declined them, though Mary wanted to live there. Their suffering together lasted twenty years before a greater one arrived—World War II. She joined the Partisans as a nurse. He preached against all the armies that passed through the village—Croatian, German, Serb, Partisan—declaring them all rapists and plunderers, which many of them were. At the end of the war he talked against the Partisans, who had executed several local Croat peasants as collaborators, and for that he went to jail, probably to be shot. My mother went there asking for him several times, not knowing whether he was dead or alive, and finally when she argued that since he had lived in America his head was filled with strange notions and he could not think straight, the police freed him.

Mary did not come back to Pavle. She could not forgive him that instead of fighting fascism, he had used his courage to offend everybody. That was the high interpretation of their divorce, which I heard repeatedly as a kid.

The communist government gave Mary an apartment near the Square of the Victims of Fascism in Zagreb as a reward for her being a Partisan. Though she could now live well, she got her American passport in the United States consulate and went back to Cleveland. I did not know what she did in Cleveland; people never bothered to tell me, nor did I ask. Just being an American was a lucrative profession.

Years later she visited her relatives in Zagreb, so my family went to Zagreb to see her. She gave me orange pencils, thinner and longer than the Yugoslav ones, which came blue or brown, and never with an eraser. Now I had an eraser, too, a whole apparatus in one elongated finesse. I stared at the transatlantic grandmother; she wore a blue skirt of a thin fabric and a string of nearly-white beads around her neck. Her hair was gray and blue and so were her small eyes, which blinked from the camera's flash that my older brother, a medical student at the time, was blasting at her. He had good reason to be so fascinated with her: when our father nearly disowned him for marrying a woman from the coast, she would send my brother a monthly stipend. Mary spoke in a funny way, slurring her r's, softening her consonants, and lengthening her vowels; she was a foreigner.

My father was vexed because she gave our family, except my older brother, no financial assistance, and helped her two sons build houses. One used the money to buy an apartment too small for his family and spent the rest on good living. I liked that uncle because whenever I visited him, he let me eat as much paté as I wished, thickly spread over warm, white bread, while at home I could eat meat only once a week and paté now and then, which Mother spread so thin that the brown bread stayed dry and barely swallowable. Uncle Ivo smoked cigarettes—the only member of our family to do so—and told me hundreds of jokes he had collected as a truck driver on his noble mission of distributing wine and brandy throughout the Federation. The other uncle (a member of the party and many bars) was Grandmother's favorite because he had joined the Partisans right at the beginning of the war, when there were few. He built a house in the suburbs of Zagreb, Dubrava, with the agreement that one apartment would belong to Grandmother so that she could retire there.

And one year she did live there. Mother, my brother, and I visited several times. My cousin showed me Mary's room, with her wigs. "She's almost bald, you know?" he said. As she had a large aquiline nose, he called her the bald eagle. He showed me her dentures in a glass, and her bracelets and earrings. Most of the grandmother seemed to be detachable; she was a composite of American products, a true industrial person. Yet to my eyes she was also folklorically natural: in her hooked nose and the wig, I saw a reflection of the American Indian culture—her wig was the scalp of an enemy, a powerful one: capitalism. We all wanted the spoils, impudently begging. She had bought my cousin a dovecote, with letter carriers. Seeing that he got so much, I asked her to buy me a tape recorder. She did. Other cousins got record players, flutes, and none of us were grateful because she was an American. The greed of her relatives who hung around her expecting money and bricks, the failure of socialism to create a feeling of community, her not getting along with her daughter-in-law (a Czech peasant woman with rabbit teeth and a jovial temperament, which apparently could become its opposite), all drove her away. "I have better socialism in America than this," she said, and left. Supposedly, she was a communist in Cleveland.

Everything American enchanted me. I would read the words on the pencil sides and memorize *Made in America*; I scrutinized American stamps and dollar bills with a magnifying glass. The dollar bill was as clean as a starched bedsheet, self-confident, almost uncreasable, washable, unlike the Yugoslav bills: the hundred and the thousand dinar notes creased; creases became cottony and oily, and slowly disintegrated, or would, if we did not tape over the folds and over variegated pictures of bosomy women harvesters bending over wheat stalks and factory workers baring their body-builder quality chests, clenching their fists, and bulging their jaw muscles, emotionally out of control, probably in hatred of the West. In contrast to this hypermasculine and hyperfeminine socialist expressionism on dusty paper, the sturdy, nearly imperishable American dollar bill exhibited a tranquil, monochromatic green gentleman (or a gentlewoman, I was not sure) resembling my grandmother, the neck wrapped up in cloth, in no need of baring anything, yet baring much to me. I could count in English, Hungarian, and German from one to ten before going to school—no achievement since this was one of the childhood games on our block. But from the dollar bill, once I understood what dictionaries were for, I learned *God, We, Trust, Great, Seal*, and the full name, *The United States of America*, and this gave me a feeling of out-distancing my neighborhood. And distance I wanted because of daily fistfights and quarrels on the block, and violent teachers at school—a physical education teacher once punched me in the jaw, knocking me, and my upper molar, out. I admired how Grandmother Mary could stay away from Yugoslavia, and I wished to do the same. Perhaps though born in Yugoslavia I was not doomed to be a Yugoslav?

As though sensing my love for geography, Grandmother Mary mailed me a world map. From the political Rand McNally map with America in the middle and Asia split in half, I learned most countries' English names. I smoked stolen Winstons and stared for hours at pink China, yellow Soviet Union, green France—all without mountains but with black rivers of ink. For politics rivers seemed more important than mountains, or they were easier to do, which itself must have been some kind of political statement of American leisure. And leisure I wanted because I'd hated work since the age of nine when I had to spend several nights fastening leather on wooden soles, hammering thousands of nails, missing, and pounding my thumb into blue pain, helping my father meet a Belgrade glass factory's deadline for wooden shoe delivery. This large glass factory saved him from bankruptcy-jail time; that a Serbian factory saved us Croats from the local communist sharks and a local factory did not reminds me that in the sixties Serbs and Croats got along.

Even more than trade work I detested the communist work rhetoric and communal work projects. As students, a couple of days a month we'd go to state farms and pick corn in muddy fields, or rake leaves in the park, or wheelbarrow gravel on the roads. Out of spite, I rooted for capitalist America in the cold war. Most of my friends rooted for the Soviet Union. I rooted for Israel in the Six-Day War, they for the Arab League, as did the whole non-aligned world; I rooted for Bobby Fischer, my friends for Boris Spassky. To this siding with the West, I made an exception in literature. I read the complete works of Gogol, Dostoyevski, and Tolstoy, and no American writers excited me as much as these. I was such an avid Gogolite that I punched a friend of mine in the mouth and cut his lip because he said that *Dead Souls* bored him. I often went through bouts of Russofilia despite my spite.

I was the only student at our high school who publicly refused membership in the League of the Yugoslav Socialist Youth—not a smart move because it cost me participation in the exchange program with a high school in Michigan. As our high school's best student in English I had been nominated to go, but now I was blacklisted as politically inappropriate, which intensified my determination to go West. Not that I disliked the communist theories. On the contrary, I enjoyed them a great deal. But I disliked the Yugoslav Communist Party's totalitarian dictatorship, with soldiers and policemen on every corner and spies in every tavern.

(That's a high interpretation. The low one: I abhorred the quasi-folk music bands with accordions, electric guitars, and gold teeth who shrieked suicidal songs through the failing audio systems of many bars. A song entitled "Jugoslavija" caused the most wailing, tears, and drunken, violent sentimentality. No wonder Yugoslavia fell apart. So I'm probably more a music exile than a political and linguistic exile, but I'll admit this only in the parentheses.)

I believed that if communism was needed, only America could make it, and I found out that Karl Marx had believed similarly. I thought the American hippie movement and communes—that's where it's at!—would create an enjoyable kind of communism, that America would manufacture communism as it did TV (which gave everybody the same images) and nuclear weapons (which could obliterate everybody).

For the time being I could not physically go to America, but mentally I could, through English—my grandmother's tongue. (It should have been my mother's tongue, but when she moved to Yugoslavia at the age of three, she quickly forgot her English and learned Croato-Slovene; there's no such language, but in my grandparents' home, there was.) I learned English everywhere, walking with a dictionary, sometimes memorizing fifty words an hour during boring sermons and lectures, but mostly I learned through rock: Jimi Hendrix ("I don't live today. Will I live tomorrow"), Janis Joplin, and Jim Morrison ("Love me two times baby...one for tomorrow, one just for today..., I'm goin' away")—without noticing that this rock music was just as suicidal as Yugo folk music. I subscribed to the *Melody Maker*, glued its pages to the walls and the ceiling, so that wherever I turned English words burst at me like popcorn on the stove. At night I listened to shortwave radio—BBC and Christian programs with apocalyptic messages of fear and trembling. The waves themselves trembled up and down and slipped out of range and hisses and buzzes startled me from nightmares as though reptiles had crawled from under my pillow. Then a John Wayne-like voice would depict the joys of the millennium. To me the millennium meant America.

In 1974 when I was eighteen, I wrote to Mary asking for a visa. She sent me the papers and enough money for the fare. I flew from Belgrade to New York, sitting next to a young woman from Sarajevo. We had such a good conversation about our vague dreams and hopes that we declared we would be friends for life, but at the end of the flight, in eagerness to get out of the JFK customs corridors into the glamour of America (cocktails of coffee stains and urine in the subway), we lost track of each other. Since this was a charter flight, we would later fly back together to Belgrade and there I would be so terrified of the Yugoslav customs police that my friend for life and I would again forget about each other, without exchanging addresses and names. Later, I would have a similar experience with many Americans: quick friendship, and quicker forgetting.

After JFK I went to Port Authority from where, I thought by the sound of it, I would take a boat to Cleveland. I was glad to find out that I could take a bus instead; on the bus a man kept shouting that he was seeing flying cows, and he felt sorry for me that I was not. Once I got off the bus in Cleveland, I saw no people in the street, only cars, and in each car only one person, and this frightened me as though I had landed in a bad science-fiction scenario where the landscape conformed transparently to one idea: individualism and isolation, as though each person were a turtle with a steel shell. A panzer.

My grandmother greeted me excitedly. "Oh my, all the way from the old country, all by yourself, my little grandson!" We kissed on the cheeks. We rushed up the drumming stairs to her apartment.

She did not have a house of her own but lived on the second floor of a family house on East 65th, south of St. Clair Avenue, in an old Slovene-Croat neighborhood. She had no car, not even a TV set, but she had hundreds of paperbacks, mostly war novels. She shared her apartment with an excommunicated Croat priest, who filled his room with altars, crucifixes, books in Latin, and incense. He was an anti-vernacularist. It turned out he spoke Croatian badly anyhow, and in that respect reminded me of Tito, who spoke a strange mélange of Slovene, Croatian, or Serbian, with German and Russian vocabulary. The priest held services in Latin to a small congregation of Latin purists in Cleveland. He constantly muttered prayers in Latin, *per omnia saecula saeculorum.*

Mary took me downtown to the May Company and proudly introduced me, her blood, to the cashiers. She walked with me around the neighborhood to meet a hundred old Slovenes. One old man wanted to give me his forest in Slovenia because he had no progeny; he thought that despite communism his old papers should be valid. I yawned. I did not come to the States to meet decrepit semi-Slovenes. I wanted to meet real Americans. And I wasn't interested in my grandmother's war memories, though she would often slip into them. I had heard enough about the damned war. There were hundreds of ugly war memorials wherever you turned in Croatia, so one more old person sentimentalizing about the heroic times made me close my ears. She talked about gangrene, worms in wounds, Ustashi, and about staying back in a hotel room with several doctors so that if there was an assassination attempt on Tito, they could help him right away. I am sure her stories were good, but they are gone. I did not listen because Yugoslavia did not interest me.

But I did try to find out about Mary Volcensek's background. It irked her when I asked what her grandparents' ethnicities were. "You should know better than to ask such nonsense!" she said. "Let the dead bury the dead. Don't you see what nationality has done to Yugoslavia? Forget it!" Considering the past and the future Balkan wars, she had an excellent point.

I visited Mary for only a month, greedily trying to soak up America, sure that I would never be able to afford another visit. I did not know this: You can leave another country to go to the States, but once you get into the States, the States get into you, and there's hardly any way of leaving. Even if you do, you carry America with you; you shower once a day, use mouthwash and dental floss, and feel guilty when you butter your bagel. I came back to the States two years later as a student and stayed, occasionally visiting Mary.

Grandmother later moved to East 55th Street and Carry Avenue, which continued westward as a cobbled street with rusting rails, flanked by old gutted foundries. Nobody walked there; the western extension of the street had died. On St. Clair, one block south, a store sold Croatian newspapers, books, and memorabilia, and down the street was a Croatian hall. Grandmother now lived with her brother, who stayed quiet and drunk on Scotch. He said nothing, so when he had a stroke nobody noticed it for days. His wife, a retired police clerk, talked all the time, smoked cigarettes, and wore miniskirts, proud of her legs. "Not too bad for sixty, are they?" she asked me as she gave us all a ride to an outdoor concert/picnic with Frank Jankovic playing polkas. She talked about all kinds of crime cases she'd dealt with in her career, and I did not listen. I excelled at not listening. When Grandmother was away, she asked me, "Have you thought of your grandmother's death?"

"No," I said.

"Well, you should. Do you know how much a casket costs? The funeral? Guess who's gonna be stuck with the bill?"

What a practical and cruel way of talking, I thought.

Mary again took me for walks around her neighborhood. She went for coffee every afternoon to the fire station at the corner. All the firemen knew her and jested with her. "She's something, you'd be surprised, things she comes up with!" I was surprised. She would not stand for loneliness. She was sociable. I guess to her firemen were like soldiers, like Partisans. This must have recaptured something for her.

For lunch she took me to a Lutheran church. She was no Lutheran, but the church had a program for the elderly. Slovenes, Croats, Czechs, Germans, chatted in their mélange of languages. As long as she could walk and take church buses this was good, better than a nursing home.

But the visit was not altogether pleasant. Once when she felt quite relaxed, she confided to me, with a voice of emotion and compassion, in English, "Your mother should have never married that brute, your father!"

"How can you say something like that?" I said. I thought this again was something political. My father had spent the war as a deserter. First he was in the Croat Regulars, then he deserted to the Partisans, then when he was sent to the front lines, he deserted the Partisans, hid in woods, and perhaps did more jumping back and forth to avoid fighting. He was, from a military standpoint, a coward, though as a pacifist he had his areas of courage. He had enough trouble with communists in Yugoslavia; now even here he got insulted. He was dead a long while, and his memory for me was a painful one. To top it off, Mary said my older sister, Nada, should never have married "that factory worker," who had six brothers. "She should have become a lady, and that factory worker made her wear galoshes and long, thick fabrics all the way down to her ankles! She was so bright, brighter than all of you, and she had to end up with that mule, permanently pregnant with his children!"

Instead of being understanding and realizing that there was probably some justifiable subtext to these statements, I put on airs. Of course, when I was leaving, I dropped them, and shook hands with her. I wanted to obey the tradition and kiss her on the cheek, but she said: "Don't bother. I am an old woman. My mouth doesn't feel good, it stinks, I am sure. And forget what I said."

In 1981 I visited her on my trip from Wyoming, where I had worked on coal mine silo construction. I hitchhiked to Cleveland. I walked in cautiously and lied that I had taken a bus from Wyoming because I did not want to disappoint Grandmother by appearing to be a bum. To her mind, I was the first of her line to attend an Ivy

League school, so the education should amount to something more than hitchhiking and a back injury that would yield no workmen's compensation. Her sister-in-law asked me what I would become— Mary never did; she probably considered it a personal question— and I said I'd studied philosophy, so a college teacher. The police clerk viewed me suspiciously, and as soon as Grandmother was away, said, "She's not gonna last. Neither is your grand-uncle. All these funerals are coming up for me! You think there's any money to inherit here? Forget it. She's spent all of it on her thankless relatives in the old country. Do you think any of them will care if she dies? Sure they will: they'll wonder whether they've inherited anything. But the little she had, it's all gone. Medical bills. She's had two heart attacks! You didn't know, did you?"

Later Mary had her third one. I talked to her on the phone. All she wanted to do was die. She quit eating and drank only ginger ale. "I close my eyes and hope I don't ever have to open them again. The last time I nearly made it, but when I was unconscious they took me to the hospital! And I had told them to leave me alone. I came to with IVs, oxygen, the works. I've lived long enough. There's nothing I need to see or know anymore. Good-bye!"

I learned of her death in my mother's letter from Croatia. It wasn't even a cable since Mother probably could not afford one. The letter took two weeks to reach me. I don't know what I was doing when the letter arrived. I know what I was doing when John Lennon was shot: I was eating a dry French baguette in a basement in New Haven. I know what I was doing when I heard JFK was shot. I was seven, yet I remember I was walking uphill past the library on a startlingly sunny morning with stone cobbles glistening between the Serb Orthodox church and the Catholic church when I saw black flags and heard JFK was dead. But when Mary died time did not stop, nor did the place freeze or burn itself, or whatever, into my memory. I was almost glad she had died. She wanted this. I did not call Cleveland. I suspected that her brother had died too. I did not wonder how much I should contribute for the funeral costs; I had nothing.

When I visited Croatia the summer after that, all kinds of distant and close relatives asked me about her money and inheritance, and I said, "What inheritance? Don't you know she had nothing. Be glad you don't have to pay for the burial." I think some of them thought I must have got everything, and in a way they were right but not the way they thought. Nobody was sentimental for her except my mother. She understood that her mother must have been poor. She never thought that everybody in America was rich. She never wanted me to give anybody any dollars. Of course, I felt the pressure to give dollars wherever I went, whenever I saw my poor nephews and nieces, but my mother said, "Don't be like your grandmother, or you'll end up like her, a forgotten pauper."

And there the story would end, I thought, but last year, when I visited my brother, a theology student in Switzerland, he made an addendum: the low interpretation of why Grandmother had left Yugoslavia. Right after World War II, while Grandfather worked in the fields, our uncle, father's younger brother, and Grandmother carried on in the house. Pavle, or perhaps our father, caught them. This was such a disgrace that Mary ran away from the village to Zagreb, quickly had her papers made, and went back to Cleveland. The uncle was excommunicated from the Baptist church and never rejoined. Our strict Baptist father may have chased her away, and for the rest of his days, he despised his brother Drago and shunned him. Nobody talked about Drago gladly. When he died half the relatives refused to go to his funeral. It was not incest but still, our father's brother sleeping with our mother's mother was adultery close enough to incest to cause the first divorce in our family history. But then, what history? Who's kept it? Traces of our ancestors vanish. So, who knows. Mary's hatred for our father could stem from this disgrace at least as much as from politics. But this low interpretation may not be true, may be just a rumor.

But after whatever brought them apart, Grandfather Pavle sent her messages to please come back. Years later he remarried but often still wept for his first wife, my mother said. He'd loved Mary till his death. His second wife had to put up with this, but she understood it. She raised him a marble tombstone in the small Protestant cemetery (he had become a Baptist in the States) near the rail tracks. My mother respected her more than her mother, for her humility and unrequited love for Pavle. Whenever the train passed that spot, I leaned my head against the windowpane and saw Pavle's stone. I remember walking in his long funeral, the oration at his grave, the feast after the burial. How sociably he had died. And how desolately Mary did.

I don't know where my maternal grandmother's grave is. I think it is in Cleveland, but what cemetery? What kind of memoirist could I be with so little knowledge, and perhaps respect, for my ancestry? One day I will drive north and look for Volcenseks (originally Volzehntscheck, Wohlzehnsheck?); maybe I will find her grave. I don't know whether there's an epitaph on her tombstone, whether there's any stone. But there's an epitaph in this for me— she gave me English and courage (or cowardice) to leave Croatia. I probably gave her nothing in return, but she wanted nothing. "Let the dead bury the dead."

My language of choice—if this was a choice—is matrilineal. Croatian as patrilineal I have rejected: I don't write in it, and now I don't even know what Croatian is since it's been changing under political pressures. It was always politicized; first it had to conform to Germanization and Magyarization, then to Yugoslavization (with Serb syntax and vocabulary), and now under the new nationalist government it's been "ethnically cleansed" to some archaic form. By now to educated Croats my Croatian appears to be a mélange of all kinds of things. Several years ago, I myself shrank back when I heard a man who could speak neither Croatian nor English. In each sentence he'd mix the two, and to understand him, you'd have to be bilingual. I've let my father's tongue atrophy. This may appear callous and unpatriotic of me, but if I were feelingly patriotic, I would be open to criticism just as well since this charge easily befalls Croats and other weak nations. (Ivo Andric, the Croatian writer who won the Nobel Prize for Literature in *1961*, considered himself strictly Yugoslav, not Croat, and he wrote almost exclusively about Serbs and Muslims; he was so little "patriotic.") The politics of language—almost as much as bad music— probably drove me away from Yugoslavia, and Grandmother's tongue attracted me overseas, and this all made me become an American, if that's what I've become.

Most language is matrilineal anyhow. *Lingua is* a feminine noun. My wife breas-feeds and teaches our son English. At the age of fifteen months he knows two dozen words. I taught him only two, *tree* (he says it as "tzi") and *bath* (as "bah"). Jeanette has encouraged him to say his first sentence: "Go-go zoo." As soon as he wakes up, he brings his little sneakers to our bed, balances them on our heads and shouts, "Go-go!" I don't bother him with Croatian even if one day he might decide to look for his roots in Croatia. I think they are in Cleveland.

SECRET SPACES
OF CHILDHOOD

The setting—Daruvar, Croatia, in the late fifties and early sixties—in which I grew up was highly inimical to the notion of privacy. Yugoslavia was a staunchly communist country, Stalinist really,
but since Tito couldn't get along with the Soviet Union, Yugoslavia
practiced its own brand of totalitarian socialism. Our ideologues
regarded privacy as a bourgeoisie disease; everything was public or
was to end up being public. What need was there of possessing a
book when you could go to the library and read one there? What
need was there for hiding anything in a society guided by the beautiful motto, "Brotherhood and Unity"? The emphasis on doing
everything together was tremendous. You wouldn't go out and run
alone; you would do it in a group, at school. You'd be geared toward
playing group sports—soccer, basketball, European handball, vol-
leyball—and hardly toward individual ones. I think Yugoslavia and
its offspring countries have the highest ratio of medals won in
group sports versus individual sports in the world.

And for me, there was an additional agency exerting pressure
against privacy: the Baptist church, in which I was raised as a member of that scorned minority. I grew up with the notion that God
sees everything, and no matter what you do and where you hide,

God will watch you.

So privacy was a disease (for Socialists) and sin and illusion (for Baptists). It was a hopeless case, not worth attempting, apparently.

And yet, precisely because both groups exerted, or attempted to exert, such total control over me, I desperately wanted someplace to hide. But before I could worry about space, I worried about time. We went to school six days a week and on the seventh, I had to be in church most of the day, listening to zealots who measured the intensity of their inspiration by how long they could carry on their sermons: we'd sit there for four hours, listening to the same lines of reasoning being repeated ten times. As if that weren't enough, we Baptists went to church every Thursday evening for a prayer meeting and every Tuesday for a youth group meeting, and these again could stretch for hours.

Perhaps because I had to spend so much time in public, I created a portable private space within me: I grew to be shy. I never let on in public what I really thought and believed. I didn't like to be scrutinized, and if anyone's gaze rested on me for more than a couple of seconds, I interpreted it as an attack aiming to expose me. It was one thing was to have the inevitable and just eye of God scrutinize me, but to have the eyes of neighbors, siblings, and uncles search through me was something else.

To make matters worse, we were a society of gazers. There were many talented spies all around, employed and unemployed. This was not simply a matter of politics, but of some remnant of tribalism, of *zadruga* (an agricultural collective of several extended families living together) that used to be common among the Slavs. The maxim, "It takes a whole village to raise a child" worked in the old *zadruga* system, and people in small towns still wanted to employ it, not necessarily with the benevolent aim of bringing up a healthy child but more frequently to discredit your neighbor's child so you'd feel better about your own. Simply put, in those still mostly non-television years, scrutiny was a form of entertainment, a continuous soap opera of a whole village or town that thrived on disclosed secrets and shame. On the other hand, the whole town braced itself against the same collective gaze that it turned upon itself. No Stalin or God could change the desperate need for a bit of private turf.

And indeed, a construction craze swept the town with the modicum of prosperity that occurred when President Tito managed to borrow a lot of money from the International Monetary Fund (IMF). Moreover, many people began to work in Germany as *gastarbeiter* with the sole aim of building their own homes. And so houses with solid brick walls laid on concrete foundations sprang up around the town. The windows were protected with solid roller-shutters that could sink your house into total darkness in the middle of the day. Of course, this all may have sprung from some kind of sensation of threat, as though another war were about to come. We constantly expected a Soviet invasion, and clearly people weren't completely wrong about that. The casualties in the wars to come in the '90s would be much higher if it hadn't been for such solid construction that could, indeed, withstand a lot of bombing.

One of the first houses to be constructed in this bunker-like mode was my father's. In 1959, when I was three years old, we moved from a little house into a large one that was one-third finished. He kept working on it piecemeal, finishing a room here, a terrace, a garage, and so on, but leaving in the middle of the house a wood-storage room. Nine years later, when my father died, the house was not finished yet. The yard went through similar construction attempts. He built one workshop, where he made wooden shoes, and then a shack and a sheep stall. As soon as he finished the stall, a new town ordinance forbade keeping livestock. Our garden was large, an acre. The whole place was a construction and work chaos. Planks of wood, sand, bricks, granite rocks, iron rods lay in piles here and there. And then, there was the large sawdust pile beneath my favorite walnut tree. The workshop hosted circular and band saws, rotary rasps, and all sorts of adzes and knives. Above the workshop was an attic with piles of neatly stacked wooden soles. So if I was to hide anything (including myself), there was no shortage of space. Whenever I did something wrong, which could result in flogging—my parents believed in a "Spare the rod, spoil the child" style of upbringing—I hid. One particularly effective hiding space was in the bales and stacks of cowhide in the dark attic of the main house. Here I could insert several wooden soles and create a hidden cave within the cowhides. I would crawl into the cave and stay still. Nobody knew of my technique.

I had many locations where I could hide, even in the public park and nearby forests. Several of us played Robin Hood in the woods south of the town. Here we'd hide swords which I made in my father's workshop, using his variety of woodcarving knives to make smooth weapons. We also made bows and arrows with reeds, turkey feathers, and large nails. Then we stole oxhide from my father and made shields out of it, stretching it on a wooden frame. There were several cave-like formations, which we covered with branches and leaves, and used as storage spaces. We spent more time carving weapons and storing them than actually playing Robin Hood, although sometimes we did manage to hold archery tournaments, and wrestling, boxing and fencing matches.

We all had our secret spaces. A friend of mine, when he moved into a large office building that was too decrepit to hold any offices any longer, proudly displayed all sorts of beams, and dark corners under the roof in the attic. At one end of the attic, his mother smoked hams, so we'd cut off very flimsy slices so she wouldn't notice that anything was missing. In small bottles, he hid plum brandy he'd stolen from his father, and this we'd sip in minute quantities, just for the fun of experiencing the burning of our throats. In a way, the more intriguing the secret spaces of your home, the higher your social appeal would be; in making a new friend, you'd try to impress him by what strange and unexplored worlds you could offer. At any rate, that was my attitude in both offering and seeking friendships. And for these explorations, we were left alone. I don't think this sort of privacy is possible in the States these days. You wouldn't leave two ten-year old boys to roam unobserved in attics and basements and then to slip into the streets and play till eleven at night in a forest. Yet our parents didn't panic, didn't call the police, didn't even worry that much. The only reproach we'd get was that dinner was prepared in vain if we didn't even eat it. Frequently, for a meal, we'd jump a fence and eat fruits and vegetables in someone's garden.

On the other hand, if you stayed at a friend's place, his mother would feed both of you, but as we didn't use the telephone there was no way to notify your mother that you wouldn't be home until midnight. And once we did get home, my brother and I didn't like to announce that we were there. We had our own tree, a large and knotty apricot, that we could climb to the second floor and jump directly into our bedroom. We scoffed at using the staircase.

Now, I think this amount of freedom that we enjoyed was possible precisely because the town was full of official and unofficial spies. The town was tremendously safe. Nearly all the boys and many girls freely roamed in the town of ten thousand (with a busy downtown, such as not even one-hundred thousand people make in the States). There were people on foot in almost all the streets of the town. I don't know of a single case of a child being stolen, abducted, or anything similar, something that's a constant fear for parents in the States. Even during the war, I remember that while visiting Croatia, I saw children walking to school, sometimes two to three miles away, by themselves or with other children. As a child, you used to live, and still perhaps do, in a blessed zone of unconscious safety over there. I remember a friend of mine in Zadar complained that the war changed everything, that now she was so nervous that she couldn't let her son leave her sight for more than a minute without her running to check on him. While she talked like that, she completely forgot about her seven-year-old, and only an hour later, when we paid the pizza bill, it occurred to us (to me first) to ask, "Well, where is Dinko?" We found him on the next block playing in the Roman ruins with a couple of other unsupervised boys, even though it was the middle of a busy summer. I don't even know of cases of sexual abuse, and talking to many of my peers they couldn't recall anything like that either. Now and then, there would be elderly single men who liked to talk to young boys, and they'd invite us to walk with them in the park, but they only talked, and talked very interestingly, without ever touching us. Perhaps because the eyes of the town were everywhere, there was hardly any possibility in public places to cross the forbidden lines. So I'd say the tremendous scrutiny that we were subjected to in the streets—sometimes you'd even discern figures behind the curtains of windows peering out and eavesdropping—created such a safety net that we could be left alone. Strangely enough, although my assignment here is to talk about my private spaces, I talk about the spaces of my generation in my town, for our privacy was of a communal sort. Best friendships were forged in these hideouts, where we smoked our first cigarettes and had first sips of brandy. Years later, many of us are still in touch.

Of course, I could remember a different sort of private space: books. I read them in corners in the attic, with shafts of sunlight hitting the page through cracks in the roof. I read Jules Verne, Alexandar Dumas, Mark Twain, and various Westerns. Well, those were certainly important, but somehow, the impression that I have when I think of privacy is that of space into which special friends could be invited for long conversations about whether God existed, what the best form of communism would be, whether we would all end up living in a commune, and about many other matters, personal and political. Caught in the crossfire between Baptists and communists, to me many basic questions were a matter of life and death, even eternal life and death. I didn't fit the church's requirements nor the party's requirements to qualify as a perfectly acceptable boy, and I had to find a way of surviving psychologically, of standing on my own, for I didn't want to end up like everybody in church or everybody in the party. I craved—and in a way created—an alternative because I couldn't completely give up faith in God nor could I give up school and society. And so there we were, with our underground alternative society, thousands of children crouching in corners all over the country, as though a bombing were already in progress.

A MEDITATION ON WOOD

We came out of wood. Everybody in the family, for generations, lived off wood. My great-grandfather also died from wood. A falling tree killed him when his son was three years old, and his son, when he was ten, took on the trade of chair-making, and passed it on to my father, who preferred making wooden clogs. My father's brother was a woodcutter. Peasants brought tree trunks into our yard, my uncle cut the logs into pieces as long as his forearm, and Father sawed them further down into orange cubes on his circular saw. Then Father drew with a lead pen profiles of clog soles, spitting to give the pen a more inklike flow. He sawed along these purple lines, and then rasped the sole's indentations into the wood, making the elevation for the arches of absent feet. For that he had woodhandled knives, and later, iron rasps with thousands of little teeth, like little hedgehogs, that rotated on an axle.

When Father's saw broke down, I carried it to Novotny. Depending on how you bent the long saw, it sang, and you could play plaintive music on it with the voices of thousands of slain trees if you weren't afraid of the sharp, jagged teeth. Novotny, a soft-spoken old man whose face I can't remember, welded the saw together with purple flames.

Sawdust spouted out of Father's workshop through a tube into the back of the shop, and the rest I carried in baskets and dumped around the walnut tree. The soil crumbled into dust, and the wood into sawdust that grew yellow and red and rotted into the earth.

Father's hair was full of sawdust. His cap was sawdusty. Our cat's fur shed not dandruff but sawdust. My nose was full of sawdust. My father's ears and brows were frosty from sawdust. When he was too tired to lift his arms, he dipped dry bread into milk and spooned honey which came from wooden hives in our garden.

In good weather we sat in the yard on tree stumps. I counted winters and summers in the cracking circles, as well as the dark years of good rainfalls and the light years of sunshine. From the dark orange centers, rays spread on all sides, cracking into the wood.

Mother chopped chicken and goose necks with a short axe over the stumps, and we ate. The blood soaked the stump, the water washed most of the blood away, the sun dried whatever remained, and the blood that built my bones and that gave me breath also entered the grains of wood and suffused it with the scent of salt.

The world had long ago entered the age of plastic, alloys, and gasoline, but we still lived mostly in the age of wood, knifing and sawing through wood as though trying to cut a way out of it. We kept ourselves warm on wood from the discarded edges of the cut soles. The wood that our father deemed not clog-worthy burned in our furnace. Even the sawdust burned in his furnace, giving a slow heat that burned with a smokey hiss.

I don't live off wood anymore. None of my siblings work in wood. We don't cut trees, we aren't frosted over in sawdust, and we don't stay in the same region of Western Slavonia as our ancestors did for generations, living off wood, rooted with the wood into that hilly root-held soil.

Life appears—sifted through my memory like light through the leaves of a deciduous forest—to have been more elemental, less synthetic, than now, although my memory may be lying to me, spinning an illusion of fall colors. I imagine that if we had been Greek philosophers, we would have surmised that wood contained the substance of the world most completely. Not that the wood would deny fire, water, earth, and air. On the contrary, it would create them: exude mists into the indigo dawn, spit out orange fire tongues, and breathe out dank, invisible, yet green, air. And when it fell to the ground, with droves of ants and maggots, the wood would open up its entrails of soil. The universe could have come out of a tree seed, growing, magnifying, and sprouting everything out of its darkness.

But as it was, we were not philosophers but followers of a religion of wood. Jesus's father was a carpenter, and Jesus was trained as a carpenter and was later nailed on a wooden cross, partly because he had not remained a carpenter. Maybe that's the Gospel of Wood: whoever leaves the ways of the wood shall be nailed and hammered.

DECEPTIVE
PLEASURES OF CHESS

In my hometown in the late sixties, a friend a couple of years older than I invited me along to the chess club, which was actually a pensioner's club populated by Second World War veterans, some of whom wore partisan caps with red stars. In the stinging smoke of stale tobacco in which you could see the weak round lamp like a moon drifting in the clouds, men lined up along the tables and slapped chess clocks. The ticking of clocks and the slaps gave you a sense of urgency, as though bombs were about to go off. From all that slapping, sometimes a walking stick which had been leaning precariously against the edge of the table would suddenly fall onto the freshly-oiled floor and startle me. I didn't smoke, unlike most kids my age (thirteen), so with all the ticking and the nicotine, I became deliriously anxious. I was terrified of making mistakes.

Sometimes I won, and often, just after painstakingly gaining an advantage, I would make an oversight, and a knight would leap and pin my rook. I envied my friend, who beat all these old men who had spent fifty years playing chess and had a grand time petting his stomach, laughing, joking. I would leave with my cheeks red, nauseated from tobacco. It was a thoroughly miserable experience, yet when people asked me what my favorite hobby was, I answered, without hesitation, "Chess."

I didn't like to play those who were much stronger than me, but I didn't like to play those who were weaker either because the victories felt empty, and I was getting worse by playing bad players. Of course, finding an equal would be best, and for a while there was a chance I would have an equal partner.

A friend of mine studied openings in books, and when we got together, we played and discussed chess strategies. Instead of opening wildly—bringing out the queen without a supporting cast of other major pieces, for example—we now followed the concept of tempi, each developed piece counting as one tempo point in the first ten moves. Good development is essential for effective attacks in the mid-game. Soon, we wanted to apply what we learned, and for several days we played. If I touched a piece, he insisted that I move it. When excited I sometimes did not control my hand enough, so that it would leap ahead of my thought and touch a piece. Sometimes I let him take back moves in exchange for his neglecting that I had touched a piece. So instead of playing chess, we negotiated our way through games, which would have been fine if we had simply analyzed various possibilities from a given position. Gradually, I managed to control my hand, and I began to win most of the games, while my friend huffed and smoked more and more furiously. On one occasion, I waited for him to make a move, but he didn't. He stared at me hatefully. I waited. He stood up and swept away all the pieces.

"Why did you do that? I had you licked," I said.

"So why didn't you make a move then?"

"It was your turn."

"No, it was yours."

"No wonder you play so badly, if you can't even remember whose turn it is."

"I would if you didn't take half a year to make a move. We have to get a chess clock."

"You are an idiot."

"Repeat that."

I did. He punched me in the chest. After gaining some composure, I returned the favor, and pretty soon we had a vicious fight, rolling on the floor, trying to strangle each other. So that was the end of that partnership of fun.

No matter where I played, I felt that undercurrent of hostility, and chess seemed to serve as a form of safe fistfight. Your nose would not be broken, but your ego might be. The word "checkmate" comes, according to Emory University's Franklin D. Lewis, from the Persian *shah-maat*, meaning "The king is stymied." It's a game of strategy, like a war game, and as such, it was totally adored in the Soviet Bloc and the former Yugoslavia. Tito played chess, newspapers portrayed him with a chessboard in front of him. He said on one occasion that he was such a good player that he never lost a game on his yacht, Galeb. Then he added, "But I never played one there." It is the only humorous thing I remember our dictator saying.

The communist bloc countries saw chess as the expression of their superiority in education and collective intelligence over the West. During the match between Bobby Fischer and Boris Spassky, I woke up early to get newspaper accounts of the games. I rooted for Fischer. Most Croats in town rooted for Fischer since he symoblized the West for us, and we longed for the West, to be let out of Yugoslavia even then, and most Serbs rooted for Spassky, as the brother Slav. In Vinkovci, I got a glimpse of Fischer, who had come to visit the chess club, and for months I felt rapturous at the thought I had been near him, as though I had obtained blessings from the Pope.

After moving to the United States at the age of twenty, I didn't play chess for five years, and when I couldn't go back to Yugoslavia because I hadn't served in the army, I suddenly redeveloped the passion for chess. I suppose for me it was a homecoming. I began to hang out at the chess club on Sullivan Street in Greenwich Village and sometimes at the chess corner of Washington Square Park. There was quite an array of characters there; a man from Israel, a former grandmaster, walked around dressed like an admiral. He had beaten former world champion Anatoly Karpov in a tournament when basically nobody could beat Karpov, but somewhere along the way, he lost his mind, and he kept strolling all around the park waiting for his warship. I found speed chess too frantic, so I sought to play half-hour games. I did not like to play games officially, but I liked to observe them at the New York Open Chess Tournament, where I saw Spassky, and the best Yugoslav player, Ljubomir Ljubojevic, who was known for having the most fabulous chess imagination and could win major tournaments, but because of his unsteady nerves could never qualify for the finals of world championships. Still, he was one of the top-ranking players in the world. I talked to him after one match. "How did you start playing chess? Did you always want to be a chess player?"

"Well, I was so restless, running out to play soccer all the time, that I was flunking out of school. My father figured that all I needed was to develop a habit of sitting to do my homework, so he taught me chess. True, chess got me to sit, but I loved the game so much that I still flunked out of school because I never did homework. Soccer was my first love, and I played on the Red Star junior team. One rainy season, we were all stuck indoors and played chess. It turned out I could beat everybody on the team, junior and senior, and that gave me such a thrill that when the sun came out, I didn't run onto the field but into the street, to the nearest chess club. That was the end of soccer, too."

In a leather jacket and with a swagger, he looked like a Belgrade hooligan, although he had just married a Spanish countess. He had deep lines along the sides of his mouth, and his eyes darted left and right. He didn't win the first prize, which was ten thousand dollars. The competition was way too tough for so little money. I looked around and saw thousands of intelligent people who were wasting their time.

I invited a Serbian chess master to live at my place for a month. I beat him the first game we played, but later he won a dozen games. He found a job as a night guard at an Italian restaurant and hung out with Roman Dzindzihashvili, a Georgian player who had been the speed chess world champion, and together they studied many openings. A friend of mine, Sasha, played chess and gambled for fifteen years in New York, living in poverty instead of working as an engineer—which he was by traininig—and practicing a lucrative and stimulating career.

Playing chess requires the ability to see many moves ahead, yet chess itself is a bad move if you want to get anywhere. At the time, in the mid-eighties, I was beginning to write fiction, but instead of writing, I spent many hours twitching in anxiety over potential oversights at the chessboard, and so I wasted my best mental energy in this ultimate game with which I was obsessed for two years in New York City. It took me a long time to become honest about chess and to admit that the game was more a mental torment for me than a source of pleasure. Now when I see a chessboard, I wince.

SAWDUST MEMORIES

Today, I have enjoyed leisure for an hour, strolling outside of my home in Shawnee State Forest in Ohio. Of course, I love forests and imagine that I am somehow in touch with my ancestors through them, and this forest resembles the forests in my native region. Just as there's evil in sloth, there's something holy in leisure. The difference between sloth and leisure, sometimes imperceptible, depends on the context, on whether enough work has been done. It was the first day of fall, to my mind, because leaves were turning and falling, while only two days ago nearly all of them were green. There's something festive in the first falling of leaves, akin to a statement that the work for the season is done, so off we go, gliding, sliding, joyfully, into sleep and other matters. Some of the happiest moments of my life had to do precisely with this sensation: the work is done, we are off.

Anyhow, today, since I hadn't worked all day, I didn't deserve that sensation, so pangs of guilt stirred, and I rechristened my leisure as sloth.

To do something useful, I went to my pile of green oak boards and brushed off mold and the sawdust from woodworms attacking several boards. As I scrubbed the wood, I went into a paroxysm of coughing out of proportion to the offense of the bit of dust. My wife, when she scrubbed the wood, didn't cough at all. My reaction was psychological, almost hysterical, and it triggered a chain of my childhood memories and aversions. In Croatia, I worked carrying baskets full of sawdust—at first bigger than myself—out of my father's clog-making workshop for half an hour every day, among many other chores that sometimes occupied most of my non-school time. As Father cut clog soles out of wood, sawdust accumulated on the floor next to his motorized circular saw. And later while he rasped the wood to fit future feet, fine sawdust flew around him in a dry, nose-scorching cloud, and he looked frosted in reddish hues, like a prophet in a windy desert. I didn't relish scooping up the sawdust, carrying it beneath the smooth-barked walnut, and dumping it there. On the other hand, I loved playing in the heap of sawdust., especially when it got wet. I could make various shapes as though in sand, and my friends and I could jump off the tree from high branches into the sawdust without harm. Still, throughout my childhood I suffered chronic bronchitis, which could have stemmed from too much fine sawdust accumulating in my lungs. Certainly, now, more than thirty years later, as I coughed in the sawdust, I could see that my body remembered that dusty labor without any nostalgia.

Carrying sawdust was a minor part of my childhood work. I had to carry finished wooden soles to the third-floor attic into storage and carry them down to the ground floor when they were needed. I had to nail leather to the wooden soles, about twenty-two nails per shoes, three times a week, usually for three to four hours. Sometimes there was pressure to meet a deadline for a village fair or the glass factory in Pancevo outside of Belgrade, so my brother, father, mother, and an assistant on several occasions pulled all-nighters. That went on for several years, when I was between the ages of seven and twelve. Near dawn, I'd be falling asleep, and the only thing that kept me awake was sheer pain: I'd miss a nail and hit my thumb or forefinger. With my sore fingers and blue nails I picked up the iron nails and hammered them into the shoe resting between my knees, my legs firmly pressed together to provide support. In the morning, my leg muscles and knees hurt, and I couldn't walk straight.

At dawn we packed the hundreds of pairs of wooden shoes into empty Brazilian coffee sacks that a large grocery store gave my father. We didn't drink coffee—although we could have certainly used it—partly because my father was a Baptist and partly because his kidneys were failing. The pain of labor was our lone source of adrenaline.

After several bouts of work like this, I detested work as much as I detested coughing and other bodily afflictions. We went to school six days a week; and on the seventh, atheists got rest, and the few of us who belonged to churches spent most of the only free day of the week in the church. During the week, what could have been my free time was work time. There was hardly any reprieve from the control of state, church, and my father's trade. I think that in protest I became lazy. As soon as I heard the word work, I groaned. But it was socialism, dictatorship of the proletariat, and even at school whenever there was a chance for us to work, the teachers put us to it. So we cleaned ditches all around the town before May Day and carried coal into the basement before winter. Most kids did not have to work at home, but many peasant kids from the hills worked more than I did. Some of them worked so much that you could see that their bodies were misshapen from it: bent backs; bony, bow-shaped legs. Still, the advantage in being an overworked kid was that you were stringy and wiry and generally fared well in fights. We fought every day, punching and strangling each other all over the school yard and in the surrounding woods. From hammering, my right arm was strong, and I had a good punch and a strong grip, which we called a "necktie." Perhaps I vented my frustrations with work in these early fights, but after the age of twelve, just after my father died, I no longer wanted to fight.

After the age of fifteen my chronic bronchitis went away. It coincided with our shutting down the business because after Father's death, my mother and a part-time assistant couldn't keep the business going.

Childhoods can be seen as happy or unhappy, depending on what angle you take, but either is an oversimplification for most child-hoods. I could easily paint a picture of misery for there was some, but overall I had much of a happy childhood, filled with mischief and play in any crack in authority-controlled time that occurred. Part of the mischief came, of course, from the awareness that things could be worse: I could be working.

But childhood was harder for Ivo, my brother, two years older than I. He accompanied my father to village fairs, where he helped set up the tent and the stands for the wooden shoes. While I carried sawdust, he carried logs. And if I fled, suspecting work in the air, my parents would look for me, calling me in the town streets. They were happy enough that I wasn't lost that I was forgiven for running away, except on several occasions when my mother beat me with willow branches and once when my father beat me with his belt. Overall, I got off lightly. If it seemed I was about to be beaten, I was not shy to scream in advance so the whole town would know a child was being beaten. I had no pride in that sense. I knew there was no way of winning, so I surrendered most vociferously, promising to be good—that is, to work.

But when Ivo hid away from work, he was flogged. It was beneath his pride to run away in fear. And he didn't want to give Father or Mother—they took turns punishing him—the satisfaction of victory. While they punished him—sometimes with thin sticks, other times with bean poles, sometimes with my father's belt, and other times with fists—he stayed silent. He clenched his teeth, and he'd rather swoon than utter a sound. Such strong will terrified me and while the beatings were going on, I trembled in fear for him. What's the point and prize of pride? He often had purple welts on his back, and several times his nose was bloodied.

Ivo grew to be thin and sulking, and he worked as our family struggled to keep the business going and to pay off debts. For a while I was thinner than Ivo, but not because of any kind of family-related stress. I had TB when I was five and six and had weakened lungs and a tendency toward bronchitis, exacerbated by incessant sawdust. But my appetite became great, and I grew to be almost husky. In protest for all the abuses, Ivo quit growing for two to three years. Vlado, our older brother, became a doctor and came to our house to give Ivo and me adrenaline shots to stimulate our appetite. He even brought us chicken and lamb that peasants gave him. He feared that we didn't eat enough since Father had become a vegetarian because of his worsening health. Later, after Father's death, Ivo pulled out of his stall and grew to be six feet tall, although I think that he never properly recovered. He is still terribly thin and looks like a concentration camp prisoner.

I cannot conclude that all childhood labor is harmful. Vlado had to work even harder than Ivo and was beaten even more. On several occasions he tried to run away from home. Once he heard that nobody could leave Albania, so he hopped on a train going south because he figured he wouldn't be allowed to leave Albania once he got there. He would be free forever. He made it once, in the wrong direction, to Austria and was returned from the border. That was a big scare in our family. Father looked for Vlado, placing notices in newspapers and traveling to visit police stations to show photographs of his beloved son. Anyway, when the police delivered Vlado home, hungry and in rags, Father didn't beat him but put him to work the very same day. There was more work to be done because of missed days.

Vlado didn't have enough time at home for homework because since the age of seven, he had to work. He wrote his homework while walking to school and read assignments on the way back. Despite it all, he was one of the best students at his school and the first one in the extended family to get a university degree, after which he flourished as a doctor. He loves work. He can relax perhaps for half an hour, and then he either falls asleep because of being overworked, or jumps up and fixes something, builds a new roof for the garage, tiles the basement floors, washes the car, or changes the oil. So he won't run out of work, he has three houses, and he keeps running from one to the other, fixing, expanding, rearranging. He doesn't drink or smoke; his addiction is work.

Generally Vlado is admired in our hometown and was even asked to run for a mayor, which he declined, I suspect, because sitting in various conference meetings doesn't strike him as real work. When I visit him, he invites me along as he works, and I must say, he looks joyful in work.

Initially, as a child, I had a joyous impulse to work. One of the earliest pictures of me, age three, shows me proudly holding a hammer in my father's workshop. And while I carried sawdust, I could look forward to Father taking a break and telling me a story that he made up on the spot. I often enjoyed being around him. Perhaps because I was pushed too far on several occasions, I have grown to detest work. But why hasn't my older brother? My explanations so far fail to be generally applicable. More is involved here. Perhaps Vlado doesn't mind work because he never got sick from it. Perhaps the root of my hatred of work is after all in my lungs, in coughing, for all that sawdust did threaten me. My body clearly doesn't like sawdust memories.

But there's more to it. Vlado, who is sixteen years older than I, worked with a young father, who had two young and strong assistants then. They used to joke and on breaks, they wrestled. If work helps children feel grown up, it can help adults feel like children, playful and frisky, if there's a good rhythm to it, and there was, according to what my older brother tells me, fine rhythm in my father's workshop. There was an atmosphere of competition, vigor, energy. My father used to claim that if he lived in America, he would turn his workshop into a large factory, but in socialism, he wasn't allowed to expand his private enterprise. He was becoming too successful for the county authorities, so they imposed heavy taxes on him, and pretty soon he had to curtail his business. To the communist clerks, he was a vestige of capitalists, the enemy of the people, particularly working people. The irony was that hardly anybody worked harder than he. He often scoffed when he saw how factory workers shirked, took days and weeks off, on pay. Soon he was allowed to have only one assistant. This embittered him. His health deteriorated; he had constant kidney and heart trouble. By that time, Vlado was away from home, at the university in Zagreb, and Ivo and I got to work with the enfeebled, aged version of Father, who resembled my image of Job. On breaks, he sweated, panted, and cursed his fate and work. He ground his teeth while working. Once he fainted at work and was taken to a hospital, where he stayed for a month. When he got back, he continued to groan in pain, but he kept working. The night he died, he worked. He worked until two or three hours before his death. Before he died, in his bed, he announced that he was finished, that he would die very soon, and calmly he wrote his will, delivered blessings to us, and proceeded to complete his work, to die. He worked himself to death.

In his stubbornness, Father resembled Ivo. He would not give up even though there was nobody around to beat him. But in a way, perhaps there was; childhood ghosts of forced family labor must have hovered somewhere around him.

Father was forced to quit school at the age of eleven, to stay at home as the oldest son in the family of ten and to work every day from dawn till dusk. The family album shows several pictures of him as a youngster, muscular, tackling wood with large wood-carving knives. He resented the fact that as the best student at his grade school, he was deprived of education and a chance to become a gentleman. He had dreamed of becoming a doctor, but there was no way. Immediate labor shackled him. I don't know how much effort on his father's side it took to confine him to the tools of torture, the trades of clog-making and chair-making. Perhaps there was physical punishment, or perhaps it was a sense of responsibility and conscience when he saw that his younger siblings depended on his enfeebled father, who had stomach cancer, and him. Still, when he inherited the family business, he worked vigorously and even joyfully until he began to lose strength, and then he suffered.

So Ivo and I adopted that spirit of suffering in work, just as Vlado absorbed the spirit of vigor and play of my young father's best years. Anyhow, my father was nearly forty years my senior. Of course, I'm merely remembering and speculating here, but one thing is for sure: I do not want to continue the lineage of childhood labor. My name is the same as my father's, Josip, without Junior to modify it, so when I visit his grave I see my name there, and his name was the same as his father's, and so on, generations back, so if anybody in the family were to continue the tradition, it should be I.

I have kids of my own and, of course, I don't plan to raise them under the tyranny of labor. But I see that my son loves work. I don't want him to work, but if he sees me hammer something, he begs to be allowed to hammer. If Mom cleans the floors, he wants to join in. If I carry firewood, he joins, and he is inordinately happy doing it. He is only five-and-a-half. Of course, if I forced him to work, I am sure he would no longer love it. When he was two years old, we had neighbors, an Italian family whose five-year-old daughter used to come to our place to play with my son, and for her it was a great game to help my wife clean the floors. She'd hop into Jeanette's high-heeled shoes and mop the floor like that, laughing. I see that in many ways children love to work. Their play, most of it, is an imitation of adult work. They are much happier with real hammers than with pretend plastic hammers. If they think they are doing real work, they feel grown-up, happy. I will see whether Joseph becomes a workaholic despite an absence of pressure from the family lineage of labor. And even Eva, who is less than two years of age, loves to sweep floors, imitating Jeanette. Will she grow to love work? Or to hate it and live with it, as I do?

Anyhow, I don't see any way for myself to shirk for long. And, I can't say that I only detest work. I'm unhappy if I don't work for a long time. But I must say, the evening after working all day, I can spend hours doing apparently nothing. "Don't just do something, sit there," as some yoga teachers say. Perhaps the most joyful moments are those of recovery from illness, and there's hardly a better simulation of that than recovery from work. When the work's done, suddenly I am hale and free. Good, this essay is over. I am free from having to write it! And who forced me to do it? Nobody. Self-inflicted punishment. In a way, when looking into my family's past, I think I got the lightest sentence, not much punishment in family labor camps, and perhaps on that account I feel guilty. I'm afraid this essay hasn't been enough labor to absolve me from the guilt for much more than a couple of hours. But, I'll enjoy them, with red wine. Or I will go and finish my walk in the woods.

DAILY BREAD

My sweating father interrupted carving wood and gave me leafy red bank notes to buy loaves. Yeasty smells drew the townspeople who were still fresh from rising in a cold dawn to the old bakery with its uneven walls and swelling mortar. Beyond the threshold, I saw naked and skinless white loaves slide into the metal oven above the random licks of flames. Soon a pale man sprinkled water from a crimson cup, glazing the emerging and tanning bread skins into polished crusts.

On my walk home I pawed the loaf, squeezed the hot dough so that it reflected my palm's lines, and chewed it, merrily filling the holes in my teeth. Then I sucked the moist bread from the holes, with a whistle.

After school I ate bread with lard that fell out of my hands and onto the pavement. With a pine branch, I scooped up the dusty lard and continued to eat the greasy bread. Ants crawled up the stick, and they carried the lard and the crumbs in a trembling line into the ground.

During the evening church service, I lifted thin slices sprinkled with white flour and washed them down with a sip of sugary indigo wine, in the Holy Communion. Then I breathed in the flour from my upper lip, the flour that the wine had not reached and pulled down.

In the musty smoke of a Czech harvest feast I listened to pork skin crackle on spits. As the sun slid down and the fires went out, the flowing, transparent bronze liquid turned into white lard. But now, while the fat was hot and translucent, old men with sun lighting their ears pushed me forward and gave me brown slices of porous bread. The bread soaked up the sizzling lard, and I ate it with purple onions, and as nausea gripped me, the coppery-red steeple above me turned green, and the green pine needles turned red.

And at home, on turquoise winter nights, several days before his death, my father, his eyebrows covered with sawdust, knifed a week-old, stony loaf into slices and broke them in his hammer-thickened fingers. When he dipped the bread in foamy milk, it drank the milk. Without using his teeth and without drinking, he gulped bread and milk and then licked honey. I ate just as he did, with my tongue, and as the bread, milk, and honey flowed down my throat, we hovered in indigo light, adrift, away from the glowing furnace, as if into a promised land.

CROATIAN JOURNAL

HOMECOMING

Crossing from Austria to Slovenia, still part of Yugoslavia in 1988, I expected my brother (a doctor in Pakrac where the Croatian war would start), who drove the car, and I would be searched by the police for undeclared taxable items. Instead, the officers nonchalantly waved us on without checking our passports. What a contrast to my entry into Yugoslavia from Austria two years before, on a bus from which all the passengers had been ordered to step down to open their luggage! Whoever carried more than a kilo of coffee was fined, and beyond the border several women in black wept loudly in a somewhat mannered way, as if ornamenting a traditional burial.

Now, about ten kilometers beyond the border, a neon sign glared DUTY FREE SHOP, the explanation, though I did not immediately grasp it as such, for our casual entry this time. I assumed the shop was for foreign tourists, in the spirit of border crossing. But having seen Duty Free shops every ten kilometers along the road, and four in one street alone in Zagreb—ironically, the Street of the Proleterian Brigades (later to be renamed Avenija Vukovar)—I understood that the government competed with the black market smugglers by opening shops in which anybody who had foreign work permits could shop with foreign currency at a decent price. The Yugoslav government thereby won a good portion of foreign currency that the Yugoslav *gastarbeiter*, of whom there were more than a million, would otherwise have left abroad. The whole thing initially struck me as liberal, but then it unpleasantly smacked of the Inter-Shops by which several East European countries desperately tried to win hard currency. I wondered whether Yugoslavia belonged to Eastern Europe, despite her claim that she was not Eastern European. During the summer Olympics in Seoul that year, the Yugoslav press reported its being clustered in hotels with East German and Hungarian press teams as an insensitive neglect of Yugoslav non-alignment.

Upon my arrival, I took a walk in Zagreb to relish the old authentic culture, a mixture of Hungarian, Austrian, and Italian influences in architecture, but neon signs distracted me, with bars invariably having English names: Kiss, Tomato, Ecstasy.

I called up two friends of mine, a couple, an artist and a teacher, and we walked on Trg Republike (The Square of the Republic). They complained about the pressures and the fast-paced, modern life of Zagreb. I pointed out that, despite our slow walk, we were the fastest walkers around, and that most people weren't walking at all but chatting, smoking cigarettes, laughing, yawning. To me, used to New York City subways—I had lived in the city for two years— and to rushing businessmen, veins popping on their foreheads from tight neckties, pushing aside mothers with babies, this looked gentle.

"But there is a lot of pressure," my friend, the artist, insisted. "Much of it is internal: How can I come up with the rent money? Where can I find my next temp job?"

They retold me the woes of the Yugoslav *gastarbeitern* economy, a story I would hear a hundred times during my stay: three-hundred percent inflation, four-hundred perecent devaluation of the dinar. Most prices were now calculated in deutsche marks.

As soon as DMs were mentioned, I offered to exchange dollars for dinars. Privately you could usually get about fifteen percent more than in banks, a nice side benefit to coming from abroad with hard cash. I thought that because of the bad economy, inflation, devaluation, and so on, now I should be able to get an even better percentage, the way I did in East Germany. My friends laughed at me and pointed at the nearest bank. "That's where you'll get the best rate. Nobody has enough money to buy DMs. To make ends meet, people have to change their DMs back into dinars. You can't buy new shoes or new clothes; yes, things are that bad."

I protested that a good portion of the people in the square wore designer clothes, looking as elegant as Parisians, and many wore tailored suits and dresses.

"The designer clothes are at least two years old from when things weren't this bad. Besides, this is Spitza. As for tailoring, sure, people do it, to save money. They do it themselves, at home."

The name Spitza comes from the German *spitz* (tip or top), bespeaking the days when it had been fashionable to name everything in German rather than English, so people in Zagreb (Agram in German) would feel they were part of Austria rather than Hungary, which they actually were for eight centuries. The city had an incredible inferiority complex historically because it had been the provincial capital of a subordinate part of Austria-Hungary and now was the provincial capital of Croatia, which was subordinate in Yugoslavia and still trying to prove through lots of foreign words its cosmopolitan status.

"People come here to show off. But just take a walk several blocks south of here."

Later I did. Most people were dressed in blue jeans made in Varazdin, north of Zagreb. A postcard I bought showing the crowded main square was mostly blue from jeans jackets and trams.

My friends and I continued to walk across the square past a fountain around which sat dozens of youngsters flinging coins and banknotes into the water. My friends looked at me with a meaningful combination of glee and sorrow. It felt strange for me to be guided, more baffled than a foreigner could be, in my home country after only two years of absence. The way my friends looked at me begged for a tacit understanding, but realizing I was not capable of it, they interpreted the scene for me. "People elsewhere throw coins for good luck because they are happy; here, it's because they are unhappy. They are throwing away their last banknotes, which couldn't buy them a scoop of ice cream." We sat down at Gradska Kavana, an old town café, and sipped cappuccino. When the bill came, I paid, and my friends did not object, although two years before they never let me pay. Obviously, they were now broke. I offered the waiter a tip. He stared at me and said, "You have already paid."

"This is your tip," I said, embarrassed because people turned around to follow our exotic conversation.

"A tip?" the waiter echoed as if he had never heard such a word. He snatched the bill, crumpled it into his pocket, and walked away, swearing.

"Nobody tips anymore," said the teacher. "And if you do, it amounts to so little that it makes no difference. The money people get simply reminds them that they usually don't get any."

This bode no good, and running into an old acquaintance several hours later contributed to the picture. Overjoyed to see me, he invited me for a beer and motioned me toward a bar, but suddenly his smile froze and scurrying away he said, "Oh, let me save money for a week; then I'll be able to come out and get a draft."

In the evening I was eager to take a walk in the dimly-lit, narrow streets of the old town, but it seemed to me I should first go to the relatives' home where I was staying to get my passport since the police were liable to ask me for my I.D. papers, according to their old habits. But an old friend who worked for the city power plant told me not to worry, that the police never bothered with that anymore. In the cobbled streets, surrounded by slightly tilting, centuries-old buildings, I had a tipsy sensation of freedom and carelessness. Behind the corners and in the park, the dark contained no potential muggers—unlike in Central Park or Bryant Park at that time—but young lovers who couldn't afford hotel rooms. The streets displayed a fortunate side-effect, from a walker's point of view, little traffic. Yes, to a visitor, this could all seem tranquil. I strolled down Zrinjevac, a graceful park with English maples. The park was surrounded by museums, tourist offices, and even an

American consulate, where I used to go to jot down addresses of American colleges when I had vague hopes of studying abroad. To my amazement, those hopes were realized: Vassar invited me to study after I had finished a year of medical studies in Novi Sad in Serbia. At the time, though I persevered in sending letters abroad, I did not belive anything could come of it. And later, this building would become an American embassy, but now, while walking by it, I did not know the future of this building but only some of its past. But what caught my attention most on this walk were the ads: SPECIAL DISCOUNTS TO GOLI OTOK. Goli Otok (Naked Island) used to be the Yugoslavian version of Siberia; just mentioning it would land you in the prison colony. In a way Yugoslavia was a mini-Soviet Union of sorts. Both were products of World War I, which both lost but, co-opted by the Allies, both reaped some rewards for being on the side of the victors. (At least Serbia did; Croatia and Slovenia, which had been on the losing side, got inferior positions in the new country). Both had republics, and in the large ones there was a Slavic majority, and within the Slavic majority, one dominant nationality—Russians in the Soviet Union and Serbs in Yugoslavia—and a half-as-numerous competing underdog nationality—Ukrainian and Croatian—with the underdogs siding with whatever invader came in against the majority group. Many Ukrainians and Croatians had collaborated with the Nazis against their big brothers. Both countries were nearly twenty percent Muslim; both had dissidents, the Soviet Union famous ones (Solzenyitsin and Sakharov) and Yugoslavia, commensurate with her smaller size, less famous ones (Djilas and Mihajilov). They both had ethnic tensions with non-Slavic minorities, such as Chechens and Albanians; and of course, they would both fall apart in *1991*. And they both resolved the need for political prisons by assigning not just buildings but sections of their countries for that function. The Soviets had Siberia and the Yugoslavs, Goli Otok, an island in the Adriatic.

As a child at school I had heard rumors about the island. At high school, having returned from my first trip to London, in an English class I read my composition about the Speaker's Corner, comparing how freely people there railed against the British government with what would happen if one were to rail against the Yugoslav government at the edge of Kalemegdan (a park with a fort in Belgrade). I had concluded that one would end up wheelbarrowing stones from one end of Goli Otok to another. The teacher, red with fury, told me that luckily for me, my colleagues hadn't learned much English and no doubt could not catch what I had just read, but how dared I, as a Socialist Youth member, express such views? I did not remind her that I had refused to enroll in the Socialist Youth organization. I was lucky she hadn't pursued the matter further; I could have been expelled from the school for my views, which of course would only confirm my views about the lack of liberty. It was incidents like these that intensified my wish to leave Yugoslavia.

And now, such stunning openness. Yes, even here, there was *glasnost*, Gorbachev-like imitation. Yugoslavia used to be far more liberal than the Soviet Union, but now it was learning from the Soviets. That did not make any sense. I wondered where that could lead. In pubs I overheard snatches of conversation; how communism was a bankrupt system, how the government should resign in its entirety. People took bets on how long the current government would last. In a satirical play, *Izlaz iz situacije* (The Way Out), Serbian nationalism, the government mishandling of the economy, and so on, were ridiculed.

As for *glasnost*, I asked the historian of Euro-Communism, Wolfgang Leonard, upon learning that he had worked in the Soviet Union and Yugoslav governments after World War II, "What was the level of chess in the Soviet government?"

"Superb," he replied. "Nobody dared open his mouth, so they all played chess, master level."

"And in the Yugoslav government?" I asked, hoping that it was even higher.

"Not so good. Nobody ever shut up there, so they played little chess, and that pretty sloppily."

Yes, people always talked in Yugoslavia, but they had to be careful what they said, and now, nobody seemed careful.

After a couple of weeks in Zagreb, I took the business train, *Poslovni Vlak*, to Vinkovci. *Poslovni Vlak* was blue, exactly like Tito's private train used to be. So, feeling privileged to enter the blue train, I sat alone in a compartment and serenely watched the countryside. Many goats grazed the turf; even in towns, goats grazed. I didn't remember having seen many goats two years before. I learned that goat-keeping was a cheap way of making sure you had milk. A ticket controller interrupted my musing on goats, asking me for a ticket, and when I told him I hadn't had enough time to purchase one, he said, "Twenty thousand dinars! An awful lot, let me tell you."

He nodded his head as if commiserating with me while I fumbled for the money.

"Tell you what, give me ten thousand, and we're quits. How is that?"

As far as I was concerned, he was the boss, so I gave him ten thousand. He pocketed the money, smiled cordially and bowed slightly in an ironic imitation of Austro-Hungarian manners. The net result was that I traveled cheaply, he made the equivalent of four hours' wages in two minutes, and the government made nothing.

I thought the practice was stealthy, but on my way back, I was disabused of that notion. The same conductor asked a man for his express surcharge ticket, and after the man pretended he hadn't known he needed one, the conductor asked him for half the amount, 3000 dinars. The man gave as told, and nobody in the compartment seemed to care.

In all this, the only change from my visit two years before was the blatancy of corruption, not its existence. The country had been permeated with corruption, high and low. Even in the early sixties, according to *Khrushchev Remembers*, Tito complained to the Soviet leader that foreign currency was massively embezzled by high-level functionaries and hidden in Swiss accounts. As a school kid, for instance, I wondered why I had never seen a friend's father, a banker, and I asked my friend about it. He replied that his father had to undergo therapy in a sanatorium for pulmonary disease. Several days afterward I read his father's name in a daily newspaper next to the magical word *embezzled* and a seven digit number. A year later, I saw his father several times in one month, after which he relapsed into an even more severe pulmonary condition, which required seven years of rigorous care. But the elastic patient completely recovered in half a year and had a brief stay in the polluted city air before needing another alpine treatment.

In the late eighties, before the trip to Yugoslavia which I am describing now, several members of the largest construction firm in the country, Energo-Invest, which built dams and bridges in many Third World countries, wrote close to a billion dollars of hot checks, cashed them, built villas, and then were caught. They did not have the sophisticated accounting schemes which Enron would devise later on, and they didn't have Tito to protect them anymore, so they got caught. The scandal that ensued shook the economy, which had been wobbly anyway. For Yugoslavia the collapse of Energo-Invest, with the consequent loss of billions of dollars in world-wide contracts, was a blow much worse than Enron could be for the United States. The collapse of the Yugoslav economy led to the blame game, and the blame game degenerated into quarrels among the Republics and into nationalism. I think that Yugoslavia first collapsed economically and the rest followed, bringing down the shell of the country.

At the time, in the fall of 1988, I did not know how swift and violent the collapse would be, but nearly everybody I talked to assured me things could not continue the way they were going. Construction workers, whether hired privately or for a government project, stole building materials which they used for their after-hours businesses, constructing their own homes or homes for others. Many people endured their regular jobs, and after hours repaired cars, televisions, or plumbing; tutored math, German, English; or translated documents. There were two economies in Yugoslavia: the official, which was reflected in published statistics, and the unofficial, gray, whose extent was hard to assess. In a way, one could imagine for a while that the Yugoslav people were doing great, that only the government was declining, and that the unrecorded economy amounted to a robust one. However, based on the official statistics with which the foreign banks worked, the Yugoslav currency was mercilessly devalued, and the low dinar resulted in lower buying power for both economies, official and unofficial, since both of them depended on imports. Thus, the misleading statistics, which hid much wealth, literally misled the economy ever lower and spoke truthfully of the country's future.

In *1988*, when, after reading about Energo-Invest and the devaluation of the dinar, I talked with people about Yugoslavia's being poor, in deficit, and how it would suffer even more when all the loans were to be repaid to foreign banks, a friend of mine, who later would volunteer to fight for the Serbian army to shell the very ground upon which we stood, said, "Yugoslavia poor? Are you crazy? Just listen, eight years ago I took out a loan in dinars, worth about 70,000 DMs, and built a large house, a fortress. A week ago I paid half the debt with 1000 DMs. I think that all I will owe them next year will be a pack of cigarettes. But I could sell the house for 100,000 DMs right now. Pretty good, huh? If people returned the real value of the loans, there would be no deficit, but why would we? This is a good deal for the people. I love the People's Republic of Yugoslavia!"

And strangely enough, just then, as he said that, the number one music hit blared from a tavern, with the singer wailing, *Jugoslavijo!* That was Yugoslavia in our native language and in the vocative case, in which you addressed people. From every corner people listened to the song, and many sang along; some wept, some gnashed their teeth. What my friend didn't know then was that his house would go up in flames, torched by the remaining townspeople in retaliation for his joining the Serb forces.

Why was the government run so ridiculously that the loans were not adjusted for inflation and devaluation in an unstable economy? The government did not want to admit the real level of inflation, and to keep up the pretense, it forced the banks to issue loans at unrealistically low interest rates. But the government finally had to put a stop to that, and now it was issuing loans at fantastically high interest rates. Of course, those dictating the low rates benefitted personally from the policy.

So some people knew how to work the system, but the majority did not seem to know. There was genuine poverty in Yugoslavia then. In Vinkovci, just before dawn as I walked to the train station, I saw a long queue of human silhouettes, some bent, many in scarves, waiting for black bread, which was slightly cheaper than the white, before the bakery opened. The black and brown scene would have made a good subject for a Käethe Kolwitz imitator.

For the decline in their standard of living, people most commonly laid the blame on the mismanaged government, and the government laid the blame on the people: bad work habits and corruption. People in Yugoslavia could not easily trust any government; for centuries they had been ruled by inimical foreign governments. The mentality of mistrust hadn't changed with the socialist regime, so the government hadn't worked with the full cooperation of the people. The unfortunate result was that Yugoslavia sank so much into debt that to a large extent it was once again under foreign control. Bureaucracies in Vienna and Istambul used to decide whether and where roads would be built in the region, and then, the IMF—American and Swiss bankers—did. The Yugoslav economy somehow always looked for help from abroad: *gastarbeiter* money, tourism, banks.

People didn't trust that the government would pay them well enough, and that turned out to be true: salaries became so low that people didn't know whether to laugh or cry at them. All the professions on government salaries lost a lot of esteem. To be a physician used to be an awe-inspiring thing, and now, a doctor told me he was opening a pub.

"Aren't you sorry to quit your job? You studied so many years for it!"

"No, I am not quitting, though the salary is for the birds. Patients bring in so much brandy and wine that I'll keep my job only as a source of booze for my bar!"

He probably wasn't joking. During my stay I had met quite a few young physicians, and none of them had stable jobs, but rather a system of rotating temp jobs with gaps in between. Not that the country had enough physicians—usually, you had to wait for half a day to get an appointment—but it apparently could not afford to employ them. And so young people no longer aspired to become doctors and engineers, unless they believed they could emigrate, but rather owners of cafés with English names and video stores.

At the same time, people grew more materialistic than ever. Before, it mattered whether you did something interesting, but now it only mattered what kind of car you drove. When people asked me what I did in the States, I said I was becoming a writer, that I had begun to publish in the journals. They stared at me blankly, and asked, "Does it pay? What kind of car do you have?"

"I don't have a car."

"Sorry to hear that," said the same friend who had built the big house on the loan inflation had diminished to nearly nothing. "You seemed to show so much promise that I expected more of you. Look at our friend Fatty." He pointed to a classmate of ours who had also returned from the States for a visit, and even from a distance, you could see heavy gold chains on him. "He and his family run a funeral parlor. They all drive Cadillacs. They are millionaires."

Even children asked me similar questions. The couple who guided me through Zagreb introduced me to their four-year-old son and told him I lived in America.

"Do you have a Mercedes?" the boy asked me.

When he learned that I didn't, he lost interest in me.

And so a strange thing happened: I noticed that the trains, which used to be always overcrowded, were nearly empty. How can people afford cars here? I wondered. Maybe they aren't that poor? It was hard for me to get the real picture. Many things didn't jibe; certainly, the salaries, which were a hundred dollars a month, and the quality of the cars did not match. It seemed the country was doing well several years before, but it was all on massive loans, and now that the loans were to be repaid by the government, the country suffered a sudden squeeze and nothing new could be made, earned, stolen.

The frustration with the economy was displaced into ethnic tensions and nationalism. During an evening stroll in my hometown's park, I heard a shriek from the dark. "I am a Serb! I am a Serb!" a pained shriek, obviously out of a well-spring of passion. Who asked him what he was? It sounded strange, drunk, stupid, to shout like that. Though this was in Croatia, I didn't hear anybody shrieking out, "I am a Croat!" At the time, the police were still mostly Serbian, and Serbs had their nationalist spree, while the Croats resented it more and more and gathered their anger and nationalism to the point of explosion. Croatia voted for a nationalist government and Franjo Tudjman in 1990, but it had difficulty introducing its own police force because the Croatina Republic was still part of Yugoslavia, and the police were federal, as were the troops, all under Belgrade's control. Anyway, in the zones with mixed population, such as that in my hometown, where there were many Serbs and Croats living together, the Croatian government introduced its own police force gradually, timidly, and uncertainly.

In the same park before the war began, in 1991, a couple of Serbs ambushed Croatian policemen and shot them. In 1988, while I was in that park, I did not know that would happen, but I could sense there was energy and hate there, almost everywhere. And there was no Tito to quell the nationalist tensions. In 1971, when Croatia went through a phase of national liberation efforts, Tito sent police and soldiers into the streets of Zagreb to club the secessionist protesters, and he jailed many leaders and would-be leaders, including the future president of Croatia, Tudjman, who'd been one of his generals, the youngest of his generals, in World War Two, and who later imitated Tito by usurping many of his villas and even the Brioni Islands. But now, in 1988, there was no Tito, and who would contain the tensions? I asked the question in a pub—the most dependable source of information—and an old friend of mine, a Serb photographer who had always loved discussing politics openly, and who always wanted to hear about the States as much as possible, said, "You are right. It would be good to have someone like Tito, and we do. Milosevic."

"Who is that?" I asked, having heard of the politician for the first time.

"A banker from New York," he replied, "who now is president of Serbia's communist party."

A Croatian man who listened to our conversation spat angrily. "That goon. He's no Tito. Nothing good will come of him."

"Oh, yes, a lot of good," said my friend. "Just wait and see."

But I could not wait and see. My alotted time in the country was up, and I had to fly back to New York to work on an old novel on an old typewriter.

AN ANTI-STORY

Now and then, I am afraid that I have lost touch with my strongest source of writing—my people, their ways and their stories—and I get the desire to visit Croatia, to plug back into my roots. But as soon as I got to Croatia in December of *1994*, with the notion of gathering material for stories, fiction and nonfiction, I wanted to leave. I stood in Rijeka in the rain among glum people and waited for the bus. I waited in Zagreb among glum people at tram stops. I could not get used to the slow and depressing rhythm of the new country, and I would probably have left right away if it hadn't been for my desire to visit my mother and my brother in Daruvar, seventy miles east of Zagreb. I had not seen them in two years. My family was glad to see me, but soon they ran out of things to say, as did almost anybody I saw in Daruvar. In whatever I heard, I did not catch the faintest glimmer of excitement, a story. After three days of boredom, I went to the train station to take the first train out of the country. Forget roots. But the rail workers, too, not only the storytellers, were on strike. I was stuck.

So when a friend of mine drove to Eastern Croatia, I went along, under the pretext that I'd see my sister, brother-in-law, and several other relatives, although seeing nearly a dozen relatives in three days had sufficed; I simply wanted to feel the road shaken into my bones through any kind of wheel. And I hoped that on the new Serb-Croat border, outside of Vinkovci, the tension would present me with story material.

South of Vinkovci, I visited Blace, a camp of displaced persons. In late *1991*, Serb forces had destroyed Vukovar, a town of *50,000*, and slaughtered in several days more than *3,000* people. Mass graves were scattered in the Vukovar vicinity. In Blace now lived *3,300* survivors from the Vukovar region; they could not go back because Serbs occupied the area. (Under United Nations' "protection" since *1991*, hundreds more Croats have been driven out of their homes in the Vukovar area.) I was sure there would be stories there.

The camp director eyeballed me suspiciously when I told him I wanted to write an article about the camp. He wanted press papers from the Croatian Ministry of Information, which I did not have. His secretary, who lost several members of her family in Vukovar, said, derisively, "He wants stories." And later, when she seemed friendly, I asked her whether I could interview her. She ran out of the room. "God forbid!" she said.

The camp director talked, dryly offering statistics about the camp before recounting how, when he was wounded and stayed at the demolished Vukovar hospital, his former best friends, Serbs who'd joined the Yugoslav army, came to jeer and to spit at him. Most of the people on his ward disappeared. He wondered how he'd managed to survive, and even more, how he would react if he one day saw one of those former friends on, let's say, a trip to Budapest. Now this potential encounter could become a story. I imagined a variation that the camp director clearly did not: that one of those jeering old friends may have saved his life, but had to jeer and spit in front of his band of murderers. Yet I was sure I would not feel like writing the story.

I walked out on the grid-like paths of the camp. Pink and light blue houses gave me a sensation of dejá vu. This resembled the Santee Sioux Indian Reservation in Nebraska where I'd worked for two years as a community college teacher. The houses were smaller, lower, thinner, but the colors were the same and so was the no-exit mood. Beyond the settlement lay dark brown and moist soil in big furrows and chunks. Most houses had little gardens next to them. Several old men and women turned the soil with spades, although it seemed to have been turned before. They dug simply for the sensation of work. Others, resigned to no work, strolled slowly, and I chatted up several of them. Most sighed and complained that it was sad beyond words not to be able to go home and not to have a home anymore. One man, who had recently discovered that he was Jewish, played with his grandson. "He's my doctor," he said of the child. "You just can't believe how joyful and good I feel around him. Whatever happened to me no longer grieves me when I see him. Of course, I worry about his future." It did not seem right to me to ask him about what had happened to him.

One man said, "What can I tell you? Those who'd have stories are in a cemetery or in mass graves. Anyway, I can't tell my stories again. They would bore me." He was pale and pink, as though his upper skin layer had been scalded and peeled. Large black spots on his face and hands indicated skin cancer. He wheezed.

I visited my brother-in-law, Kornel, in Vinkovci, two hundred yards away from the new Serb border. He showed me how he had bricked the hole from a Serb howitzer which hit the base of his house and how far he'd progressed with building a red-brick chapel in his yard. During the siege of the town of 40,000, he was among the 4,000 who stayed in the city and among several who stayed on his block. Perhaps his faith had given him courage, but the war had exhausted him. He had stomach cancer. He was diagnosed too late, and the cancer had spread to his peritoneum. He'd grown thin, his hair white, but he appeared all the nobler for it, spiritual, beautiful. We sat down, and he ate bacon, slicing it with a Swiss knife.

I said, "I thought your stomach was taken out. How can you eat this?"

"It agrees with me. I know that I can't digest it, but what's the difference now? My tongue likes it."

Then, with my nephew Ben, I went to Vagonsko Naselje (the Train Village), where 133 refugees lived in the Vinkovci train station's rail yard. This used to be one of the largest train stations in the Balkans, with lines from Munich and Athens, Budapest, Sarajevo. But now the station was desolate. On one side track sat coaches of an East German train that did not meet the reunited Germany's standards. Each coach, divided into three apartments, was equipped with little oil stoves and chimneys that stuck out the windows. When it was hot outside, the refugees were hot inside; when it was cold outside, they were cold inside. A thin young man invited us inside and prepared us Turkish coffee, unfiltered muddy coffee with spoonfuls of sugar and no milk. He used to work for a restaurant in Opatija as a cook. "I'd do that now, too. But there are no tourists. I'd like to cook for the village, but...." He shrugged his shoulders.

"So what do you do?"

"I've written a book in verse."

He showed me his green notebook filled with handwritten blue capital letters, then closed it and recited for half an hour about his region, Slavonia (not to be confused with Slovenia). He hardly ever mentioned Croatia. (There's little unity in Croatia and even less in Bosnia. Croats from Herzegovina have seized most of the power, and others have withdrawn into their regional identities. Serbs, on the other hand, have the motto, *Samo Sloga Srbina Spasava.* Only Unity Saves Serbs. Inability to get along is probably the usual plight of the smaller and the weaker.) I don't remember much of the poem because I was mesmerized by the rhythm and rhyme. "Here, after an air raid, we stand in the wind—plastic sacks flapping along our knees—and wait for foreign aid." After every stanza a slow groan came from beneath a white blanket on the bed. There was a ruffle in the bed and beyond the sheet a gaunt gray head with sunken lips.

"That's my dad," said the poet. "He's dying of cancer. His stomach was taken out." Many people with latent cancer would never have developed cancer if it hadn't been for the war. The war anxiety broke people's defenses, and cancer took over, like the weeds which swallowed the train tracks outside the station.

"And the rest is about my personal war experiences," the poet said, as though that should be less interesting. "A publisher in

Zagreb said they'd give me money for this. Other people have visited and talked about deals, but nothing has panned out. A German t.v. crew came here and filmed me to death. They made money off me. Everybody's here to make money," he said, and stared with his large hazel eyes at my lips, obviously suspecting that I was trying to turn his words into green paper.

Perhaps concluding that no matter what, it was still good for him to speak out, he continued to recite, quickly, nodding his head. He mentioned rivers of blood many times and other clichéd figures of speech. I wanted stories of survival, passion, love, and not patriotic clichés.

But it fascinated me that the man wanted to know the poem by heart and believed in performing it in a rhythm; though he did not measure the lines on the page, the way he recited them created a meter. He displayed the Balkan-oral-tradition mentality, according to which you are supposed to be able to tell long stories from memory in meter. It did not matter that he wrote the poem first: he wrote it to speak it. Most of the oral tradition evolved out of wars as epic narrative poetry dividing people into good and evil, friend and foe, mostly foe. The meter set a tempo to which you could march. Oral tradition must be one of the causes of the Balkan wars. Serbs relentlessly recounted the Kosovo Battle, where Serbia was defeated by the Ottoman invaders, as well as other heroic defeats, in teary, nostalgic, and intoxicated tones. Serb oral tales—one prominent story in the 1980s was about Muslim Albanians impaling a Serb man on a broken bottle—raised Serbian feelings of outrage against Muslims and Croats. And now this man in front of me was lamenting in the same Alexandrine tone about Croatia's loss of territory. Each war spawns its laments, which all seek revenge.

While listening to the poet, I was impressed by the poetic component of the Balkan macho mentality. In the States, poetry suffers the image of being effete, over-refined, and male poets try to restore their self-image of manhood by heavy drinking bouts and by organizing men's movements. In the Balkans, no such problem. Radovan Karadzic, the hawkish leader of the Bosnian Serbs, has published two collections of poetry. The father of the current drive for Greater Serbia is Dobrica Cosic, a novelist and poet who was nominated for the Nobel Prize and is a much better writer than Vaclav Havel and an outright fascist. Cosic was president of Yugoslavia in 1992. His narratives educated Milosevic and contributed to the Serb war campaigns. In response to Serbia's aggression, President Tudjman, a nationalist writer of history books, rose to power in Croatia, and in Bosnia, Alija Izetbegovic, author of a book about the Muslim vision of society, became the president. Writers lead the Balkan wars. I think this is instructive: since most literary enterprise is limited to a single language, usually a national language, writers are liable to become nationalist. This simple thesis is worth examining in an era of ethnicity and multiculturalism. Writers become ethnic heroes, which is great as long as we talk about emancipation and liberation. But how about when liberation turns into oppression of other groups? The world is being Balkanized partly through how the world handles its storytellers and how the storytellers handle the world. Of course, I could equally argue that too many people's silence is the root of all evil, and it probably is, combined with the few people's story-making.

Now the problem with making epic poetry is that exaggerations occur to fit the metered pathos. So while reciting, the train coach poet showed me his ear. He said, "See. Chetniks beat me with rifles and knifed my ear off. It hung by its skin and bled a creek of blood, but I got to the hospital soon enough, so it was stitched together." He flapped his ear forward so I could look at it, and I did not see a scar, but I know enough about my tendency toward skepticism to doubt my doubts.

Perhaps the poet's ear has healed marvelously well. I admired the poet, after all. He spoke in an uneducated peasant fashion, as many people do in Slavonia, and I found this authentic. Clearly, he did suffer during the war and still suffered in the limbo between war and peace, in poverty, with cancer of all sorts around him. That he could fight his circumstances, his post-traumatic stress, by creating a long poem, that's absolutely terrific. He handled the Balkan creeks of blood very well. But he partook of the mentality, the disturbing mentality, of the Balkans, the kind that makes us all who come from there unreliable. Very few journalists entrusted with covering the war in the Balkans are Croats and Serbs. It's better to send somebody there who knows nothing about the region, and who'll give you an impartial account. Or is it? So far the reporting from the former Yugoslavia has been, on the whole, superficial and repetitive. The journalists seem to take several simplified and unverified historical "facts" that they pick up from Yugoslav and U.N. diplomats and other journalists, and repeat them.

I decided I would not write a story abut my trip. I forgot the poet's name. I lost his pictures. I forgot the Blace director's name. Though I taped the director, I gave away my cassette recorder to a friend in my hometown. But you can judge for yourself how good my word is. Two months later, on a snowy afternoon, I sat down and could not resist participating in the tradition of writing stories. I'm tempted to imagine that this is an anti-story, a kind of postmodern minimalism. But my accounting of the places where I could have found stories but did not find them may be only a form of Slavic nihilism and spitefulness and a poor excuse for my reluctance to participate in the regions's no-exit sorrow.

Postscript

In 1995, because nearby Serbs occasionally shelled Vincovci, Blace and Vagonsko Naselje were taken apart and their residents resettled to other camps farther west.

My brother-in-law, Kornel, died of stomach cancer in March of 1995.

GUNS OF AUGUST

In August of 1995, I again returned to Croatia to see my family and to gather materials for stories. In the past three years, two uncles, an aunt, and a brother-in-law of mine died, all of them obscenely early, and although I could not say for sure that the war killed them, I believed that war anxieties critically weakened their defenses. My sister and a nephew were severely wounded but they recovered. I was eager to see the living relatives because at this rate in several years there would not be many of them left to see. While I'd rarely visited before the war, since the war began I've visited almost every year.

I was also eager to look around and see for myself what was going on because I could not trust the media. It was not only a vain curiosity that drove me: I wanted to collect material for my fiction. "I don't need a writing program. I need a war. If I survive, I'll have enough stories to last me a lifetime." That's what I wrote in a story several years ago, before the current Balkan wars. A good deal of literature in the former Yugoslavia deals with wars; the novel *Bridge on the Drina* by the Bosnian Croat, Ivo Andric, who wrote in Serbian and won the Nobel Prize in literature in 1961, to a large extent deals with wars. Miroslav Krleza, the second most prominent Croat writer, has wars lurking in his writing. The Balkan oral epics stem from wars. If you come from the Balkans, war is the paradigm of story-making.

I flew to Zurich to make a connecting flight to Zagreb, but my flight from Zurich to Zagreb was cancelled. I flew to Ljubljana in Slovenia and came to the Zagreb airport on a bus. The airport is south of the city, less than fifteen miles away from the Krajina Serbs' lines.The Krajina Serbs had cluster-bombed Zagreb in May, when Croatia reclaimed the Western Slavonian Serb enclave. Now Serbs were about to take the safe-haven of Bihac in northeast Bosnia. If Bihac fell, Bosnian Serbs would reinforce the Krajina Serbs and then perhaps take the southern coast of Croatia. The Serb forces were several miles away from the coast from where, whenever they pleased, they shelled the ancient city of Zadar. For Croatia, this was the "To be or not to be...."

And for Serbs, this was the to bomb or not to bomb, and now I was within their range. In *1991*, a hundred thousand Croats had been expelled from Krajina, dozens of villages were razed to the ground, and thousands of people were slaughtered, some in massacres.

When Croatia was recognized as an independent country, it was still basically unarmed. If the Serb armies and the Yugoslav Federal army (the fourth largest army in Europe) had been more adept, they could have swept most of Croatia in a month. But things have changed. Over a four-year period, Croatia captured a lot of weapons and bought even more on the black markets of Eastern Europe and Russia.

Now on our trip from Zagreb east to Western Slavonia, Boris, my brother Ivo, and I drove on the Highway of Brotherhood and Unity, which used to link Zagreb and Belgrade. We passed dozens of dark green trucks with somber recruits in them. Once we left the highway, we enjoyed looking at the countryside in the full summer, lush with plums, vineyards, corn and wheat fields alternating in small strips of colorful land going in different directions, with winding paths and streams, groves of beech, willow, and fir. It was sunset, when nature comes to rest, and people do not work the fields, but even so, there were unusually few people outdoors. In the center of each village was a bus or several green trucks and people in camouflage, waiting.

"Where are they going? Krajina?" I asked.

"Most of them to the east, to fill the emptied ranks, and the professional soldiers will attack Krajina," said Boris. He used to work as a liaison officer for the county office of Daruvar and the United Nations, and his opinions were usually accurate.

Next morning, because of my jet lag, I woke up early and walked in my hometown. There was hardly anybody out at 6:30, even though this was a town of early risers. When I got home, I watched TV: a well-groomed man playing the piano and singing, in English, with a pained face, *Stop the War in Croatia*. The media used to play that song in late *1991*, when Croatia was under attack by Serbia.

Then the TV showed a long letter by Tudjman, addressed to the leaders and the people of Krajina, and each paragraph started with a dependent clause. "Because you have not accepted our peace proposal... Because you have continued to bomb our towns and villages... Because..." And the conclusion was: "Croatia has decided to undertake measures to restore order." *Redarstvene mjere*, the original said. The term was used in school when I was a kid, for school discipline. In the letter, Tudjman invited the Serb populace not to run away but to remain and enjoy the benefits of full civil rights in Croatia. It took me a while to realize that the letter was a declaration of war.

Then the TV showed the images of three dead swimmers in Dubrovnik, victims of Serb bombing from the hills. As long as Serb forces occupied high ground around many Croatian towns, it was impossible to live normally: the message was loud and clear. Four years of negotiations with Serb leaders and international mediators had yielded no substantial concessions from the Serbs, which basically affirmed the primitive principle "Might is right" and which left Croatia cut in half, with a stalled economy and more than three hundred thousand displaced persons. Croatia now apparently had enough might to be right.

That morning, August 4, the TV and the radio reported that Croatian forces had been advancing toward Krajina since five in the morning. And again, the song *Stop the War in Croatia* was broadcast. Without a strong attack from Croatian forces, the low-grade terrorist war would continue, so in the long run broadcasting the song made sense, but it still struck me as odd that the side that was undertaking a large blitzkrieg offensive should be broadcasting songs of peace. I was following the program, and I did not trust it.

From the BBC radio news, I could gather that there was an international diplomatic effort to dissuade Croatia from attacking Krajina. That struck me as strange, for if Croatia quit the offensive, Serbs would take the northwest portion of Bosnia, with potentially a large massacre of Muslims in Bihac, where people were starving to death anyhow.

On the Croatian radio and TV, there was very little information about how the action was going. I was tense. So were my brother and his family, and my mother. Although I hadn't seen her in half a year, when she commented on the news—and she was in the habit of commenting after every sentence—I could not resist asking her to be quiet so we could hear the news and not her opinions. Everybody was tempted to comment, but we all had to practice the discipline of listening, hoping to hear what was actually going on.

The radio gave announcements by various foreign embassies advising their citizens to leave the country, even those that were in the north of the Adriatic, far away from the fighting. Many people scrambled to leave that day. Some friends of mine from the coast left right away. My brother and his wife were tempted to leave for the sake of their kids. We interpreted every siren as an air-raid warning until we learned it was an ambulance or a fire truck. Our mother was not fazed by all this. She was far more anxious about whether we would find her food too salty.

The radio advised people against walking in the streets unnecessarily and especially against gathering in groups. Movies were cancelled; the soccer season which was supposed to start was cancelled. My friend Boris and I still went to a hot springs pool at the local spa and listened to the radio. The radio announced that the Serb defense lines had been penetrated in thirty key strategic points along the seven-hundred kilometer border. No mention of casualties. What if thousands of soldiers were killed? What if the penetration of Serb lines was a Serb tactical maneuver to entice Croat soldiers into traps? I must admit, I was not used to Croatia winning.

Later my brother and I talked with a Serb friend of ours at a coffee shop. Zuco acted as the U.N. liaison with the Serb community in Western Slavonia. He said information was censored on Croatian radio, although until several days before, the radio had been largely accurate.

"The first report was that Petrinja was encircled and about to be taken by Croat forces. Before the action, the line of separation between the Serb positions and Croatian positions was zero kilometers; now it's two kilometers. Serb lines have not moved back. So interpret this as you like." He was basically saying that the Serbs were advancing, not the Croats. He obviously believed in the Serbs' might. But as he joked and talked with another Serb, an engineer who'd gotten a job at the local brewery despite his ethnicity, he spoke softly so that I had to lean in to hear what he was saying, and a lot seemed to be said quite obliquely. Croats used to talk like this in Yugoslavia, and in our town when Serbs ran the police department, the secret service, etc. The tables had turned. Still, Zuco somehow seemed self-confident: he believed he had the correct information. He was certain that Boutros-Boutros Galli was a friend of the Serbs because the Copts were basically similar to the Eastern Orthodox and Serbs were Eastern Orthodox. And for Serbs it was difficult not to believe in their superiority in the former Yugoslavia.

The Krajina Serbs had for decades bragged that they were the best fighters in the world. They had received an amazing amount of arms from the Yugoslav army; supposedly many people slept with hand-grenades below their pillows, and some peasants had tanks in their barns. The Serbs had veritable fortresses along the front lines, thousands of bunkers, hundreds of tanks. Recently, Serbia had sent several top generals to organize the army, despite Milosevic's supposed noninterference. Although their way of waging war— encircling towns and lobbing shells into them for months—did not in any way seem to be heroic, I still did not know them not to be good soldiers. The tide of the war could easily turn. In Bosnia, whenever an offensive against Serbs started, they retaliated and not only recaptured the lost territory but advanced beyond it. On a Serb radio station that afternoon, I heard the lyrics of a song, "God, defend our Republic of Serbia, and let it grow bigger than ever." If the tide of the war turned, with help from the Bosnian Serbs, they could be quickly in my town, too.

In the evening, I went to a restaurant in the park, "Terrace." At an outdoor table sat a blond man with a mustache. For sixteen years I've come back to my hometown every few years, and although many things have changed, this man still sits at the same table in the same restaurant. He looked no older than the last time I saw him, five years before. "Hi, Byeli," I said. "Everything changes, but Byeli stays the same. It's nice to see."

"I wish I could agree with you. You see, in *1991*, during the very first bombing of Daruvar, shrapnel hit me in the head and in my knee. It went into my brain. I had brain surgery, and it's a miracle I am alive, my friend."

"But you are still here."

"Yes and no. My mind's not what it used to be. I have anxiety attacks all the time. Feel my hand."

I felt it. It was wet.

"I'm a nervous wreck. I have nightmares. I can't run any more. Who would have expected in a peaceful town like ours that these thugs from the hills would start firing. I always got along with everybody. Incomprehensible." He used to joke and laugh, but now he just stared straight ahead.

Daruvar was not absolutely safe. A couple of days later, Bosnian Serbs flew over in their jets to terrorize the Croat population. There was an air-raid alarm just as my brother, his family, and I were leaving Daruvar by train. The jets bombed a chemical factory nearby, in Kutina, where Boris and I had driven a day earlier. The Serb intention may have been to create an ecological catastrophe in Croatia. The factory was damaged, and the roads to Kutina were closed for several days, but a major spill did not occur. The Serb jets bombed several towns, killing a dozen people. The Croats shot down two planes, and after that no more flights occurred. The Serb style of warfare was counterproductive because over the years, just as the Croatian morale and support for the war would slacken, Serb terrorism would motivate people again to support the war so that type of terrorism could not happen much longer.

The way Serbs surrounded cities and bombed them—for example, Sarajevo—served hardly any military objective except pure terror. The terror motivated the Muslims to fight. Serbs held Sarajevo under siege for more than three years; if they wanted to occupy it, they should have tried rather than using this ancient Greek style of encirclement, which could go on for ten years like the siege of Troy—minus the heroic deeds, which could later be added, in the oral tradition of exaggeration.

I should have been happy that the war was going on because I could gather stories. But where? I could not gather them on the front. To begin with, I had no journalist's assignment and no papers to go there. Anyway, this was not a journalist's war: Croatia prohibited journalists from visiting the front lines. Croatia wanted to pattern the war after Desert Storm, and indeed, the government named this operation "Storm." A journalist who tried to visit the front lines was killed, perhaps in the crossfire. When I watched foreign journalists on TV, most of whom spoke no Croatian, or listened to incompetent interpreters at press briefings at the Hotel International in Zagreb, I did not envy them. If staying in expensive hotels passes for war reporting, I have no reason to admire it. And if you are dissatisfied with the reporting from the region, now you know the reasons: censorship and journalists' lack of genuine knowledge of the region. The only way for me to get to the front was to volunteer, and even then, since I was not trained in the army,

I'd probably simply get to hang around some desolate place in Eastern Slavonia. Anyway, I thought the most interesting stories need not be those involving direct battle reports.

Talking to people, I gathered bits of true stories, like this one, which did not cheer me. I called my sister, Nada, in Vinkovci. She told me that just that day the Serbs had launched close to a thousand shells on Vinkovci. Shrapnel had hit Nada's neighbor in the head, and he was taken to a hospital. Two people were killed, twenty injured. Nada's husband had recently died, and her son—who used to sing "God protect Croatia while I defect to Austria"—was recruited. So she stayed indoors alone, took tranquilizers and aspirin, and lay in bed with a fever. She said she'd rather be struck by a bomb than go to her cramped and wet basement. She ran out of bread but did not dare go out of doors because she had once been struck by shrapnel in the liver and nearly died. In the evening, a neighbor who had not been struck in the head—but risked it—drove to the bakery and got enough bread for the whole street. He gave her a loaf. Maybe there was a story to this, but it was too close to home.

And I heard another story from a Muslim friend. An old Croatian woman, who lived alone with her canary, accommodated a Muslim woman refugee in her home. The Croat insisted that the canary cage stay above the refugee's bed. The newspaper, which served as the cage floor, was soaked and broke. Bird droppings fell on the refugee. In the morning, when the old woman went to the farmer's market, the refugee opened the cage to clean it and to put a plastic mat on the floor. Through an open window the canary flew out of the apartment When the old woman got home, she was crushed that her feathered, life-companion was gone. She threw the refugee with her things out the door. I should be able to start a story from this, but for now, let it stay as an anecdote. For me it's an anecdote. For the refugee, no doubt, it's not.

A friend who'd avoided the draft told me that all the soldiers he knew loved to go to the front. The first time they were sent there, none of them did, but now they even volunteered because there they had the best time. The men from our town were sent to the Sava River, along the Bosnian border. They took along miles of fishing line and thousands of fishhooks. During the day they shout across the river to the Serbs, and the Serbs make offers for the fishing line because they love to fish in the Bosnian brooks. When they agree what to barter, our guys take a boat to their side or the Serbs come to our side. Our guys get looted VCRs and even gold fillings—taken from corpses, of course. All the soldiers I know adore corpses because they can get rings, necklaces, and gold fillings. Dead soldiers especially are prized because they have probably looted too; they may have pocketfuls of gold. Anyway, at night these guys who trade goods and jokes during the day, shoot at each other with machine guns and mortars. And in Herzegovina a while back, when Croats did not have enough tanks, Serbs sometimes rented the tanks out to Croats for several hundred German marks a day. Rent-a-tank.

Upon hearing this story from the Sava River, Boris and I drove close to it, south of the Highway of Brotherhood and Unity, in Western Slavonia. We came to a point where we could go no farther. There were several buses with idle Croat soldiers waiting for the word on where to go next. An acquaintance of my friend lived in a house along the road where the buses waited, and as we drank coffee with him, two soldiers joined us. One drank plum brandy, but the other one wanted to stay sober. He refused even coffee so he wouldn't get too excited. The sober soldier asked us to punch his abdomen to see how disciplined he was. And he talked about a Croatian soldier from an elite unit. "He stole ten white goats of mine. When I complained to him, he first denied it but then returned four of them. I wonder, where are my other goats? I'm taking him to court. I hope he hasn't eaten them..." That's all I heard there. Maybe I could imagine the rest.

All around the country, people told each other entertaining and laughable things about the war, for a reprieve, I guess. But while I was in Croatia, stories and reporting were actually far from my mind. I was tensely following what was going on. Maybe now that Croatia was capturing more arms, securing more territory, there would be a balance of power, a basis for true negotiations. If one party is much stronger than the others, you can't forge a good peace. The balance of power worked in the cold war; it was the basis of the cold war. Croatia, Serbia, and Bosnia-Herzegovina should rather have a cold war, than the hot one. So when the reports came about the fall of Knin and then the fall of Petrinja, and it was clear that Croatia was winning ahead of schedule, optimism and euphoria swept the country.

I took a train ride to Rijeka—or rather, I wanted to. The train was cancelled: the line passed along the Krajina region. I took the bus, and it went right to the Slovenian border. Krajina had squeezed the rest of Croatia all the way to Slovenia at one point.

In Rijeka, where I stayed with my sister Nela and brother-in-law, Zdravko, at night I heard machine gun fire. It was only some drunks celebrating the victory.

Almost everyone I talked to supported the war except a playwright I met on the island of Krk. He lamented that the Serbs were leaving the Krajina region as refugees.There would be a hundred thousand people bearing a grudge, raising their children in hatred of Croatia, and a decade or two later, a new generation of Serbs would be ready to fight wars and commit acts of terrorism. "This is not good," he said. "More should have been done to protect the civilians and to treat them well."

"What nonsense," said a friend of mine, Ranko, who worked as a power plant technician in Zagreb. "They were invited to stay over and over again. It's their own propaganda that scared them."

"That's not quite accurate; more should have been done to reassure them," said the playwright. "Publicly they are invited and privately, terrorized."

"Listen," Ranko said, "no matter what happens, they make stories up to hate us as much as possible; there's no way of assessing if their migration will intensify these stories. It could act differently, to sober them up, disabuse them of their myths of being great soldiers. If they quit seeing the army as a great career, they will menace us less. They can come back anyhow if they want to."

"Are you sure they can?" the playwright asked.

Overall, I could detect little sympathy for the Serb refugees, although an in-law of mine, with apparent pity, said, as we watched refugees on TV, "Just look at them. A bunch of poor peasants, old men and women, scared, lost. There's little to feel triumphant about when you watch them."

Ivo Banac, a Croatian historian, told me, "Very few people in Croatia realize that Croatia loses something with the Serbian exodus."

Most Croats saw justice in this exodus: Krajina Serbs had nearly all voted to secede from Croatia, they had supported the military action against Croatia, and rejoiced in their victories and even in atrocities; many of them had plundered Croat villages in the Krajina region.

After such prolonged Serbian aggression against Croatia, Croats could not see the refugees as defenseless. Many of the Serb refugees still had weapons. An article in *The New York Times* reported how the Vojvodina Serbs, in Serbia, were nervous about the Krajina Serbs arriving there, because the Krajina Serbs had weapons, and the Vojvodina Serbs didn't.

A distant relative of mine who worked as an anesthetist for Croatian commando units told me how his friend's task was to give bread to departing Serb refugees on a road. As the friend handed a loaf of bread into a truck, an old man from inside the truck shot him with a handgun. The friend fell and died. The incident was not reported in the international press.

The Croatian police protected the refugees so they could depart peacefully; Croatia wanted that to be known abroad. But near Sisak, a crowd of Croat civilians attacked a column of departing refugees with bricks and clubs. This was broadcast abroad as a common occurrence, and many Croats were upset about this. They said,

"Look, our people had to leave on foot, and here we feed them, give them free gasoline, let them take away their cars and weapons, and they talk about us clubbing them and killing them. If we wanted to kill them, we would. They can even stay with us if they choose to. Nobody will harm them, despite all that they have done."

It was probably true that many Serbs could stay. They could also come back and be protected by the constitutionally-guaranteed equal rights for all the ethnic groups in Croatia. I talked to a Serb colleague of mine—we had gone to school together. He had lost his job as a history teacher. Before the war, it was a problem for Croatia that history was taught by Serbs and they presented the story largely in favor of the Serbs. So Croatia wanted a new crew of history teachers, and he was fired. But he appealed his case, and on the basis of equal rights for all ethnic groups in Croatia he got his back pay. He did not want to move from his hometown, and he tested the Croatian government's promises and found them to be true. When I saw him, he invited me into a pub, where we drank red wine with another Serb who'd recognized Croatia as his home country and did not lose his job. My school colleague told me that he had invented a variation on Rubik's cube: a Rubik globe. He wanted to patent this in the States and asked me to help him; we would split the profits and become rich. I did not react to this. I did not believe that any puzzles that were not computer-based had any future, but I did not discourage him from feeling optimistic about his project.

On a walk, my brother Ivo and I ran into another Serb who had stayed in Daruvar. He said that he stayed despite some harrassment. The police took him into custody and interrogated him. "I usually don't get scared with the police," he said—and of course, he had no reason to get scared before because the police, who were mostly Serbs, did not bother Serbs. "But now I saw that the Devil took all the joking away, and I had to answer their questions, where I was at what time." It seems there was a Serb war criminal who shared his name. "It took five hours or so, until they discovered that the person they were looking for had a different birthday than mine. And somehow I am still in the records, so at all checkpoints they bother me."

The man was happy to see us because we used to talk often. I suppose he felt a little alienated from the new Croat-centric society and was glad to see Croats who spoke with him freely.

"A middle name would be useful, see. I don't know why we never get middle names," I said. "In the States, we use middle names to minimize confusion. Russians do it, too."

At any rate, I could see how being regularly mistaken for a war criminal could make you feel uncomfortable and why you might not like to live in a place where you were liable to be searched. And later, when I read in *The New York Times* that Tudjman claimed that the offensive was so swift and successful that many Serbs did not have enough time to gather their dirty underwear before they ran, I could easily guess what Tudjman's feelings about the refugees' departure were and how much the refugees might feel welcome to come back.

I talked to several more people. They were eager to talk about religion, astrology, spirituality. I overheard conversations, some about beatitudes and other spiritual issues. That sounded bizarre to me because years ago when I wanted to talk about religious issues, people laughed at me. Now a friend of mine, at the end of an evening, complained to my brother, "You should have talked to me about religion. Why didn't you? I'm upset with you. Here, you're getting a doctorate in religious studies, and you keep it all to yourself." It was true: my brother had gone to Princeton to study theology. But Ivo was shocked at this. He said, "Come on, don't you remember that years ago when I did talk about religion, how bored and bothered by it you were!"

I visited Zagreb during a Virgin Mary holiday—I forget exactly which Virgin Mary it was—and was surprised to find out that there were at least a dozen of them, a whole pantheon of Virgins. People walked to mass, the television stations broadcast prayers and church songs, and loudspeakers outside the church broadcast sermons. Suddenly the country was very pious. I did not remember it as such.

Churches used to be empty. Of course, it was against your career goals to go to church, but even so, many people had no career then and they had no career now, so why weren't they religious then and why were they now? Since I was raised a Protestant, I could not appreciate the Virgin Mary business, but my friend Ranko said, "Look, this is more egalitarian than the Protestant approach, which is purely patriarchal and sexist. You neglect the feminine aspects of religion; we don't." He was amazed that as a Protestant I should be so averse to the mass Catholic exhibitions, and he claimed that one of the major sources of Nazism was to be sought in Protestantism. Since Protestantism failed to create a community and actually splintered communities into several churches, which would keep splitting into more communities, the only way to have an identity was ethnic and racial. Therefore the Germans embraced racism, Nazism, as a way to form a large community. There were some leaps in logic and over-generalization in this, but there always are in such attributions of cause to religion. For example, many people see the current Balkan wars as religious. Far from it, I think, since hardly any people practiced religion before the war. Now they do, but it may be mostly a surrogate for ethnic identity and ideology.

After the holiday Zagreb looked more energetic to me than ever. The young men who were not recruited walked straight, quickly, and most of them were lean. From everywhere you could hear techno music and rap. There was an aggressive pace to the city. This was no longer a city on the brink of defeat but on the brink of victory. Even the civilians had a militaristic edge to them. I was watching an ethnically purged Croatia: from the pre-war population of 550,000, the Serbs now numbered about 200,000. And because of the war, the tourists stayed away, so that nearly everybody I saw in the streets was Croatian. The city gained in self-confidence but lost in many other respects. The folk music played on the radio was now from Croatia only; the shows on TV were mostly Croatian and American. The diversity of the society had obviously declined, and in some ways the culture was impoverished. The mixture of Catholicism and techno music in a fast, mechanical march did not charm me. On the other hand, this was a reaction to the excessive Serb militarism. Croats, including me, used to malinger as much as possible. Few Croats wanted to be soldiers or kept guns at home, while the Serbs pursued military careers and Greater Serbia, from which Croats and Muslims would be expelled. Greater Serbia would stretch to Zagreb. I suppose some kind of karma was at work: the militaristic Serbs pushed Croats into becoming more militaristic than the Serbs. Since there are more than twice as many Serbs as Croats in the former Yugoslavia, Croats must compensate through good military training. Israel became the Croatian military ideal: a small country well armed, with close ties to the United States.

Zagreb used to be gray and sooty brown and actually, outside the center and several fashionable areas, still was, like a browning black-and-white photograph from the Second World War. Now, while the Sheraton Hotel was being built, the house fronts had been painted in light green and orange colors so that the city would not look too drab. Supposedly, the hotel provided the neighborhood with free paint and labor to do this, because if the district looked clean and colorful, clientele would be more attracted to the hotel!

I may be wrong about Croatia's loss of multi-ethnicity. Croatia had hosted about 200,000 Muslim refugees from Bosnia; and the Muslim-Croat confederacy, if it worked, would culturally diversify and enrich Croatia. Before my departure, I looked for a pair of boots to buy as a present to my son, Joey. In a store run by two refugees—a man and a woman, who had run a similar store in Derventa, on the other side of the Sava River in Bosnia—I found a pair of leather boots. When the man found out that I lived in the States, he was enthusiastic. "That is the only Western country that supports us. When you get there, tell the Americans that we thank them and that we love them. Don't forget that! The Brits and the French, they have betrayed us. We are tired of their empty and cynical promises. But we believe Dole and Clinton. Without America, we could not survive." This was before the NATO bombing in Bosnia. The shopkeepers must be ecstatic now. They were appalled when they found out that I did not teach Croatian to my son, and that I did not plan to move back to Croatia.

"Why not?" They said. "That's your *rodna gruda* [the birth bosom, literally; the term used for the native place]. As soon as the war is over, we hope to go back to Bosnia, breathe our air, drink our water, be free and cured from nostalgia and sadness." We talked for nearly an hour, and they were happy to see the American Express card that I used to pay for the shoes. Americanophilia. I am not sure Americans are ready to be loved by Croats and Bosnians but that love is coming. I guess America can deal with the long distance love more easily than with the hundred thousand more exiles who would come to live in America were the war to last much longer.

I flew out of Zagreb on Croatia Airlines: the airport was now safe. The Serb lines were in Bosnia, no longer anywhere near Zagreb. At the airport, the security guards were several smiling young women with bleached hair. The country did not look like a country at war. In the plane, there were many Croatian high school kids on to an exchange program with the States. They read books in English, talked, smoked. They were surprised when I showed them the no-smoking sign. I told them to get used to signs like that before getting to the States. I wondered how many of them would return to Croatia and how many would, like me, become Americans. Before, since Yugoslavia was inhospitable to Croats in many ways, many Croats preferred to remain abroad. There are four-and-a-half million Croats in Croatia and just as many in diaspora all over the world. This may change; the Croatian government pleads on the radio with the Croatian emigres to come back and help build Croatia. But that, too, is propaganda. I did not feel welcome in my former home, and I knew that the government was full of tricks and lies.

As soon as I was out of the country and could think more clearly, I realized that I had just undergone an involuntary study in human nature: What do you believe when you are in a country at war, feeling threatened? You believe almost anything the generals say on TV or radio, and you hope that the side you are on wins. You root for your team, and just as football fans don't notice any foul play on their team's part, you don't notice it on your party's part. I knew the liberation war would not be entirely clean but partly a campaign of revenge and terror, both individual and organized. How do you find out who was a fair fighter and who a war criminal? Certainly many at the top of the government should be questioned. At that moment, I wished I could have been at the front to see precisely what had hapened. But at least Croatia was free—or was it?

COUNTRIES
WITHOUT BRIDGES

Where does the Balkan peninsula begin? Answers to this question vary and have less to do with geography than with politics. If you look at the map, you will see that the width of the peninsula where it connects with the rest of Europe is greater than the length, if that makes sense. Years ago at the high school in Daruvar, Croatia, my geography teacher, an elegant Serb lady who colored her hair blond and chain-smoked, used the absurdity of the width being greater than the length of the peninsula to claim that the Balkans were not a peninsula and should not be considered a region, either. The concept of the Balkans, according to her, was an imperialist, most recently, Austrian, swindle, to claim territorial unity in order to gobble up the area.

If you ask Hungarians where the Balkans begin, they point to their border with Croatia; if you ask Croats, they point to their border with Bosnia and Serbia. Prince Klemens von Metternich, a famous 19th-century Austrian statesmen, claimed that the Balkans began on Landstrasse in East Vienna.

If you asked me on my recent trip where the Balkans begin, I'd tell you way up north, in Austria. Once, in a bar in Vienna I was conversing with a couple of jovial men. When I told them I was from Yugoslavia (this was years before the fall of Yugoslavia, so I didn't say I was from Croatia), one man said, *"Jugoslawe—doch ein intelligenter Kerl!"* ("A Yugoslav, but despite that, an intelligent guy.") I didn't know how to take that. Was it a personal compliment and a clear insult to my country and thus also an insult to me? He kept smiling and tapping me on the shoulder and offering me another spritzer, but for me the conversation was finished. He probably hadn't noticed that he'd said anything offensive or unusual.

A black friend of mine told me that when he studied for a summer in Vienna, he occasionally went into a public sauna. One time, a man said to him, "Boy, is it hot!"

"Yes," my friend agreed.

The man looked at my friend's skin and said, "But to you that must be normal. You don't feel it, do you?" My friend is sure that the man didn't mean anything racist; he was actually attempting to be friendly and chatty but just couldn't help himself.

Fourteen years after experiencing that national slur in the Viennese bar, a friend of mine and I were driving a car through Austria on our way from the Frankfurt Airport to Zagreb. In Werfen, south of Salzburg, Jon and I took a break from our long drive. Werfen lined up on a hill along the Salzach river, beneath a wonderful castle on a cliff. I hoped that not only would we have a place to crash but also to bask in the *wunderschoen* scenery.

Every house displayed flowers on all the windows. Jon joked that they must have flower police. If you fail to put out your flowers and to keep them in perfect health, off you go, to jail. One house had kindling wood piled incredibly neatly as though it were a permanent structure, a thick wall. Austrians lined up their woodpiles more carefully than we built houses in the States.

Behind a church, there was a sign, *Unsere gefallene Soldaten, 1939-45.* It was not hard to guess on what side and for what cause the soldiers had fallen.

Since there weren't many tourists, finding a room to rent should be no problem, we were told in the tourist office. However, Jon and I were rejected at several places, so we tried a large *gasthaus* where, although there were no cars parked in the yard, the hostess told us in sweet tones that all the rooms were rented out.

A man from a house that had turned us away earlier met us in the parking lot, amazed that there was no room. "But there must be room here!" he exclaimed. After a pause, he said, "Are you from Israel?"

"No, why do you ask?" I said.

"You sound like somebody from there."

Perhaps my Slavic accent in German, with hard consonants, reminded him of Yiddish.

We kept our search for accommodations, and this man, smiling, kept reappearing in all sorts of locations, pretending to be helpful and perhaps being helpful but all the same, watching us. I told Jon the contents of our conversation, and since Jon had a pierced ear, he thought that in this conservative place people could take us for a gay couple from Israel.

As we walked on the main street to the hotels, our last resort, we passed by several cafés where old Austrian men sat and drank spritzers. What had they been doing in World War II? Who knows. Perhaps we were being followed as potential Nazi hunters.

We rented a room in a large hotel and no doubt got the worst one. Our room slanted downhill and, not surprisingly, someone above us must have had diarrhea as the toilet kept being flushed.

Before sleep, for supper I went to a restaurant. *Weiner Schnitzel menu, 95 shillings*, said a chalked sign.

All right, I thought. I'm in Austria. Among Goths, do as the Goths do.

"What would you like to drink with your meal?" asked the waiter.

"*Mineral wasser*," I answered, and then, thinking that the water in the Alps should be drinkable, I said, "No, just regular water."

The man brought mineral water in a tiny glass. I didn't complain that he had disregarded my correction.

"Would you like another glass?" A waitress, a younger version of the waiter, asked, eyeing my shoes as though I should clean them.

"Yes, plain water please."

It took about five minutes for the white cloud in the glass to disappear. When the bill came, I was charged for two glasses of mineral water at two dollars a glass, more than beer cost there. I protested that the second glass was plain water.

"What do you think?" the waiter said. "That we work here for free? That, too, was fine mineral water, without gas."

"Nonsense, tap water with a sediment."

His daughter wept. "We've got to make a living! They all think it's easy, that we are here just because we like to bring out water and food! Well, we don't!"

When I looked around, I saw that people were looking at me suspiciously, and I got an uneasy feeling.

Werfen. The name of the town means *to throw*. I know what place not to recommend. Werfen, Oestereich: Oester Reich, Eastern Reich. But then I thought it was premature to draw conclusions about Austria or to generalize my unease about the town to the whole country. I felt a bit guilty on account of so swiftly forming a prejudice, thinking: Here I rush to generalize a limited experience to dismiss the whole country, to be phobic about it, xenophobic, more precisely, and then I'll complain that the country is xenophobic, and thus I'll participate in the vicious circle of prejudice and detestation. And sure enough, now I do complain that the country is xenophobic, although there are, no doubt, many fine individuals there. And I have met several fine Austrians. One gave me a ride when I hitchhiked in Germany in 1980 and took me to a restaurant afterward to treat me to a fine meal. And one, whom I met at an anti-nuclear rally in New York City in 1982, lent me her apartment in Vienna for two weeks and left to go into the country, trusting me with her telephone. She told me, however, that her grandmother still loved Hitler and prayed in front of his picture in her bedroom.

And so, when I think of Austria, I swallow, and the bad chlorinated taste of tap water, rather than the freshness of mineral water, comes back to me.

Anyway, the Balkans, whether a peninsula or not, does start

somewhere, and Jon, a photographer, and I, began to feel the tension the closer to the Croatian border we came while driving through Slovenia. At the border, the Slovenian customs officer asked us whether we carried any weapons.

"What a ridiculous question," I told Jon. "The Slovenes are still worried that Croats are smuggling weapons."

The Croatian customs checkpoint was a mile after the Slovenian; I had never seen such a gap between two border points. Here, in 1997, Croatia and Slovenia still could not agree where precisely to draw borders; in some places, their checkpoints were three miles apart.

Later on that night, on the blacktop highway which used to be named Brotherhood and Unity, I was driving 140 kilometers an hour, already a stretch for our Opel Corsa, trying to pass a truck in the slow lane, when an Audi tailgated us, flashing its lights. I moved over to the slow lane after passing the truck. The Audi driver slowed down when I did; I slowed down further, so did he. It seemed a silly game, and I was about to flip the driver a bird sign when I noticed a long-faced, balding man with protruding eyes, shouting. A woman with a perm sat on the passenger side, and she leaned back to clear the space for his arm, which held a heavy gun, probably an Uzi. We were driving in parallel, not watching the road but each other, and he had a third eye, gazing at me with a large, hollow pupil that could annihilate me. This is absurd, I thought. He could shoot for no reason, and what could I do about it? The man kept shouting. Perhaps he had waited for the bird sign. As it didn't come, and he had made his point, his car darted forward. To use a shabby metaphor which could have been more laden and leaden for me, he drove off at the speed of a bullet.

When we got to my old hometown, which for nine centuries had been a Hungarian town, Jon and I were still pretty agitated. Although Jon had decided not to drink because of a heart condition, he asked whether there was any wine and gulped two glasses of it. My nephew Damir, also a photographer, visited us, and he admired Jon's Nikon with telephoto lenses. I told Damir about the highway madman, and he said that sometimes people shot at each other fighting for parking space in Zagreb.

Then we heard that a man had thrown a hand-grenade into a bar in Daruvar after someone in the bar refused to step out to fight. Nobody was killed, but some people lost eyes and limbs.

So what is the rest of our trip going to be like? We now had good reason to question traveling in order to write stories and take pictures. Several years before, a Hungarian woman of letters, Sára Karig, who had spent six years in a Siberian camp, answered my question as to why she didn't write travelogues with, "I don't even understand Budapest, where I've lived for fifty years. Why should I pretend that I understand Istanbul?"

I agreed with her but what is there but impressions and idiosyncrasies? Statistics? Articles in *The New York Times*, written, in the case of the former Yugoslavia, almost invariably by people who don't even know the native languages? On the internet, where anybody can post any information or fabrication? All that plus impressions could contribute to some kind of understanding which, indeed, couldn't be worse than no understanding. We have given no understanding enough chances.

Of course, from one incident with a gun there was no point in concluding much about Croatia. Whether travel made any epistemological sense, though, didn't matter; we were in the middle of it. We had one assignment: to write a travel piece on the Brioni, Tito's islands, for *The New York Times* travel section. (The article never got published there since it was not pleasant enough; in the meanwhile Perri Klass wrote a pleasant article about the Croatian Adriatic.) Therefore we drove to the coast, via Zagreb, past the still-damaged Karlovac (a town on the edge of the former Krajina, where I had served in the student military service before emigrating to the States). A military vehicle had broken down, and a dozen soldiers hitchhiked; some pissed along the road. We drove to Vodnjan in Istria, several kilometers away from the coast, where we would go on to the Brioni.

Boris, a childhood friend of mine, hosted us in his narrow and tall house, with his nephew, who, at seventeen, in the first days of the war in 1991 in Daruvar, lost his leg when the Serbs in the hills lobbed shells into the town. The nephew's mother was killed; shrapnel hit her in the neck and severed her head. The nephew's luck was that at the moment of explosion he was bending down to draw water from a water pump. Shrapnel flew over his head but got his leg. He owed his life to water. That day, he, chubby from the lack of exercise, sat with us and talked about cars. That night, not knowing his story yet, I was startled to see that his leg was missing below his knee.

Vodnjan was not a tourist town despite its charms and resemblance to Provencal towns: narrow, cobbled streets, stone buildings, crumbling stucco,, a cramped shop with wine that you could draw for eighty cents a liter. A man sitting on the stairs close to the shop said the wine was good for your blood. It had helped his wife after the doctors no longer knew what to do with her. "Why don't you buy some and drink it?" he said. "You'll love it."

"So that's the wine you drink?" I asked.

"No, I don't drink at all. Never have. That's one personal failing I have."

The wine from the hill town, Motovun, tasted like Beaujolais Nouveau, only better.

Jon, who told me that because of his heart medication, he could not drink much, was so overjoyed with this pure-tasting wine that he finished two liters in one sitting, as did I, and we went out for more. He had already suffered with me; I had sleep apnea, bordering between moderate and severe. In sleep I stopped breathing forty times an hour, sometimes for up to a minute, which I would follow with loud gasps and choking sounds when not with regular snores. So perhaps Jon rejoiced mostly to find out that he would have a room of his own without these jolting sounds. Still, I worried for him. So when I woke up, after many awakenings, pretty late, around ten in the morning, and heard no sound from Jon's room, I was sure that he had died of a heart attack. Why did I buy wine for him? Maybe that was a good way to go. If he's just dying, how do you resuscitate? Mouth-to-mouth with a bearded fifty-year-old? Where are the emergency numbers? The nearest phone? Then he woke up hale and said he looked forward to more wine in the evening.

We went to the local café, Arca. A young man told us that his parents used to be hippies; they dropped acid, smoked pot, and then drove to Graz to listen to the Stones or Jethro Tull. He, too, would like to be a hippie but couldn't afford the drugs and concerts. He planned to emigrate to Austria to "affirm" himself (*probiti se*, literally, to penetrate oneself, meaning, to penetrate the scene and launch a career; in Croatian, too, the expression lends itself to sexual innuendo and cynicism). He would penetrate the scene, in writing. He didn't know German but expected to find someone, most likely a beautiful young woman, who would translate his prose for free. He would stay with various friends of his, depending entirely on his charm, in which he believed so much that he talked only about himself. Although it was August, he didn't plan to work until January, his envisioned emigration date, because life would be hard enough after that. He said he'd dropped out of high school because he was a genius and the teachers morons. I asked to see one of his manuscripts, of which he said he had tons. Gladly, he obliged me and as I read, he smoked and scrutinized my face for signs of intelligence. The manuscript, written calligraphically, was full of grand metaphors to describe his surging emotions about himself. He didn't even mention the wars.

But the café was pleasant with its slow rhythm. At the large square, Narodni Trg or Piazza di Populi, the pink, palatial county office building changed to purple when shadows stretched over it. Many people watched the streets stealthily from behind their blinds. With the streets so narrow and houses jammed together, there was absolutely no privacy here, not even for the observers. The whole country was and had been like that, a damned federation of spies. I remember that hardly anywhere, right before I left for the States in 1976, could I have a normal conversation because people would point at their telephones, insinuating that they were bugged.

On the main street of Vodnjan people shouted from before dawn until late into the night, in Croatian and Italian. The street signs were bilingual—and Vodnjan's name is also Dignano—as was nearly everything in Istria, which used to be Italian. The Italian neo-Fascists still aspired to annex this region; many Slavic and Italian Istrians would like to join Italy, as well, believing that they would prosper. However, Italy itself can barely stay together.

Jon and I drove south to Zadar, where an acquaintance of mine, Estella, who studied Croatian émigré writers, invited us. I came there willingly, although I was one of the subjects of her dissertation and hadn't known whether she would dissect me with her questions. She didn't. She believed in the death-of-the-author approach (luckily, not literally), and she believed that all you needed to find out about a text was in the text. She'd read my books and that would do.

Estella and her husband, Vinko, let us stay in their rented weekend home because foreign tourism was still down. He lived off tourism, ferrying people from the coast to the almost untouched Kornati islands, a fabulous archipelago. He said he'd organized the first trips to the islands twenty years before for German tourists. He'd give them all the wine they wanted, and when they got to the islands, he and his crew would carry their naked and unconscious bodies and pile them up on the sand, like beached tuna. Every three days, he'd have to change the crew because they got exhausted from too much sex. "Oh my, that was hard work," he said. "I couldn't do it anymore."

Vinko and Estella lived in an apartment in the walled part of old Zadar. Zadar used to be an Italian town, and as such was severely damaged by Allied bombing in 1943 but was beautiful, nevertheless. So even now, Estella and her husband grew angrier when they talked about the Allied bombing of Zadar than when they talked about the Serbian siege. Of course, at the time, they still could not predict that there would be an Allied bombing of Belgrade.

Staying in their retreat, we ate grapes from the vines and figs from the trees, even the green ones that bled milk. Jon smiled beatifically and relaxed as I suppose only someone on strong medication for controlling blood pressure who had also drunk young wine can be. He judged people according to how relaxed they were—a healthy way, I guess, of considering people if you must stay relaxed for your heart. Bibinje, the village next to Zadar where we stayed, looked like a Santa Monica marina: a thousand boats, yachts, sailboats, docked neatly. But a little away from the marina, there were still many demolished houses. You couldn't easily tell whether the damage came from the Serb cannons firing from the hills or from Croatians planting bombs in the houses of the Serb officers who had left to participate in the attack on Zadar.

In downtown Zadar, the white stone pavements were so footworn that they reflected the light and glared in the sun. The church of St. Donat was built on Roman ruins; stone from pillars and monuments bearing Latin inscriptions still lurked in the foundation. The church, built in the ninth century A.D., resembles the Hagia Sophia in Istanbul in its round, Byzantine architecture. Zadar was at the crossroads of East and the West throughout its history.

Already a new archeology was taking place with ruins from the recent war which, simplistically, could be described as the Roman Catholics versus the Orthodox playing out the old religious schism. After the Serbs had surrounded the city and shelled it for two years, some buildings were damaged, some patched up, and the old concert hall, supported by a system of beams, seemed beyond repair.

Stella said that still, when she walked to the marketplace, she made sure to keep the fortified walls on her right to protect herself from guns in the hills. She had to remind herself that the war was over. Her son had a facial tick. Stella said, "You know, I'm so nervous for him that if I don't see him for a second when he's out with me, I panic."

"That's how we are in the States, all the time," I said.

We sat down for pizza, and Roko, her son, disappeared for half an hour, and Stella didn't notice. I pointed that out to her. Slowly she looked for him and found him in the next street, playing on a wall of ruins. Lifestyles here could not be changed by wars easily.

After spending three days in Zadar and Bibinje, Jon and I wanted to be serious; enough blue sea, beaches, tourism. Time for Bosnia and Herzegovina.

The drive along the green Neretva River and orange plantations felt festive. Road vendors cooled bottles of drinks in small water fountains of their making. I did not know when we crossed from into Bosnia-Herzegovina. The border should have come and hadn't. After a while I realized that we had crossed it. That was in sharp contrast to what I expected: a country at war, heavily policed. But the Herzegovina part was in the south near the Croat border and was Croatian, and in this manner the Herzegovinians wanted to say, "We are Croatia." There were pictures of the despotic Croatian President Tudjman along that road, more of them than we had seen in two weeks of our stay in Croatia. The word was *Zajedno*, "Together." Which can mean here, "Let us be Croatia." Since Croats had constituted only seventeen percent of Bosnia's population before the war and now only ten percent, and they were the only ethnic group that did not control a city (Serbs had Banja Luka; Muslims Sarajevo, Tuzla, Zenice, and most of Mostar), they would be scared to have no protector and did not want to be separated from Croatia.

We passed by several devastated towns. Near the road stood a new black gravestone marked JOHN ERIK, a journalist killed in Bosnia. All around the road, there was a putrid smell of decomposing flesh. Could it be human? Or animals that stepped on mines? Sooner than we expected, we were in Mostar, and we parked on the western side of the Neretva. I thought the river was the dividing line between the Muslim quarter on the east and the Croatian quarter on the west. I walked over the military-engineered bridge, whose wood thudded whenever cars drove across. Jon had a party taking photographs; the town was so ugly because of the devastation that it was bound to be fertile ground for a photographer.

Along the river were many buildings with grenade holes. Nobody smiled. Many people knitted their brows, and they'd make only sideways eye contact with me. It was Saturday, and I couldn't get any Bosnian *dinars*. We crossed back to the western side, which I'd heard accepted Croatian *kunas*, sat at the first café by the bridge, and ordered a double espresso and a mineral water. Next to me at another table sat a grim man with pursed, thin lips, thick black beard, and an aggressive way of looking around him. When the time to pay came, I offered the *kunas*. "Oh, no, I can't take that," the waiter said in Bosnian.

"I heard I could use it here."

"Not here."

"Is there a bank around?"

"Yes, several blocks that way. Go past the SFOR tanks (International Stabilization Forces), and you'll find a bank that'll change that and that'll be open."

"Aren't I on the western bank?"

"Yes."

"But isn't that...."

He interrupted my asking, clearly understanding the next word would be, "Croatian," and said, "No, a few blocks off."

Luckily, I could buy some German marks from Jon. The waiter returned the change in German marks. He was quite polite but tacitly reminded me that I had made a *faux pas*.

Croats and Muslims hated one another here. The Croats had finished off the bridge, which the Serbs had damaged first. One explanation for destroying the bridge was that the bridge had served for smuggling weapons to the western side, where Muslims were advancing. Now I saw that both banks of the river were under Muslim control. I could see the Croatian point of view, just as I could see what an atrocity it was to destroy the graceful old bridge. Two days after our visit to Mostar, a car filled with explosives blew up in the middle of the Croatian quarter, destroying nearly one hundred apartments, wounding more than fifty people.

The drive to Sarajevo was surprisingly smooth. No checkpoints. I found out that according to the *1995* Dayton Peace Accord, no sides were allowed to set up checkpoints. In Jablanica, on the way to Sarajevo, many people sold trout along the river.

In Sarajevo, along the Miljacka River, wedged between steep mountains, there were signs indicating minefields after Princess Di's visit. The press reported the princess' death widely, along with interviews with mine victims who had met her.

I couldn't immediately find my nephew's address in Sarajevo. Toma worked as a Baptist minister. I asked a policeman, who greeted me in the old communist way, *Zdravo* (Hail!), to my *Dobar dan!* (Good day!) He gave me precise directions but directed me into a one-way street against the flow of the traffic. I pointed that out to him, and he said, "Fine, if you feel like driving around five blocks, go ahead." We drove around because I wasn't sure he wouldn't ticket us if we drove against the flow of the traffic. Later, I saw that people all over the city drove in the opposite direction on one-way streets; they sped, scaring pedestrians.

Several people mentioned to me that they were wounded. Not, it turned out, in the war but in the traffic. Driving in Sarajevo was a miserable experience, with people leaping in front of your car every thirty seconds; cars not yet completely ahead of you darting into your lane; the exhaust of diesel trucks exploding into your face.

We went out with Toma and his wife, Lidija, to walk on the street Ferhadija, in the old town, Bascarsija, in a pedestrian zone. The prayers sounded from several minarets; we were surrounded by five visible ones. We walked into the yard of one mosque, where people were taking off their shoes and washing their feet in a fountain. When a young man found out that we were not Muslims, he gave us pamphlets, trying to convert us.

We went back into the cobbled street, admiring the windows of old shops, goldsmiths, bakeries, all arranged beautifully, with ornamental wooden frames. Soldiers from several nations from Stabilization Forces and women in traditional long skirts and shawls, wrapped up even around their chins, walked, pale and clearly unexposed to the sun, while others walked in tight miniskirts.

We met a mild-mannered Iranian. He said he was a calligrapher, a Christian. His passport was expiring, and he couldn't get another one because the Iranian embassy knew that he was a Christian—he was converted in Damascus. "If you aren't a Muslim, you aren't an Iranian citizen," he said.

The Baptist church in the old quarter didn't wear a cross; inside, it had a fish sign. "Why?" I wondered, and Toma told me that it wasn't clear that the Muslims would tolerate a new cross on a building in the city. We attended a service, with many people from charitable organizations and from the international police force. A couple moved from the States to retire in Sarajevo because, they said, it was God's will: Sarajevo needed them. Although he looked absolutely square with a crewcut, and so on, the man joked, played the guitar, and was generally as carefree as if he were vacationing in Waikiki or as carefree as a stoned hippie. Who knows, maybe a hippie soul got trapped in a Baptist body.

We visited the town park and the Bogumil cemetery there, where we saw gravestones with Glagolitic inscriptions. (The Bogumils, a 12th century Christian cult, were persecuted by the Catholic Church as heretics for their dualist views.) Children playing soccer used the gravestones as goal posts. We saw some graves between houses in Dobrinja, a suburb close to the airport. The entrance to the tunnel from which people could go underground to the airport was between several large socialist-built high rises. Here white goats grazed among lacquered wooden graveposts.

Not far from the downtown area, we saw half a dozen people, including women in shawls, taking bricks in wheelbarrows away from a nearly destroyed house to a lot half a block away, where another house was being built. When Jon wanted to take a picture of them, as an image of Sarajevo reconstruction, the women swore at him, and shouted, "Go to Pale (the Serb headquarters, a mountain resort town above Sarajevo) and take pictures there, scumbag!" They threw stones at us.

Afterwards, Jon and I talked to several young people, including Haris, a Muslim rock musician, who worked as a construction worker, and a Serbian woman who had left Sarajevo during the Serb siege and studied law at the University of Pristina in Kosovo. It didn't bother her that only Serbs were allowed to study in the middle of a province that was ninety percent Albanian. It seemed bizarre; she genuinely seemed to be a pleasant person, yet these basic social injustices didn't faze her. I wondered whether chauvinism had infected her so deeply that Albanians didn't count as humans for her. When I studied medicine in Novi Sad from 1975-1976, many Serbs expressed contempt for Albanians, saying, "They multiply like rats; there shouldn't be so many young alive among them!" This seems a perfect prelude to ethnic cleansing, where murder would not be murder but belated abortion. During Serbian student demonstrations, the parols weren't anything progressive and inspiring, but, "Give us arms! Let's go to Kosovo!" Even then, many Serbs wanted to attack Kosovars. Sasha, an otherwise reasonable Serb friend of mine, grew irate whenever Albanians were mentioned and on one occasion, on Third Avenue in Manhattan outside of a Russian bar, with his penis hanging out he chased an Albanian friend to piss on him. Even when he was sober, Sasha claimed that our Albanian friend was not really Albanian but Kosovar, clearly, to his mind, the lowest category one could be.

Nevertheless, the young I interviewed all seemed amicable. They thought that Bosnia should stay together as one country, and that Bosnian identity was stronger than Muslim, or Serb, or Croat, in Bosnia. The Bosnian Serbs, for example, thought they had more in common with Bosnian Muslims and Bosnian Croats than with Serbian Serbs.

But let the Sarajevans speak for themselves:

Haris Ganic, 26. Muslim.

JN: What kind of work do you do?

Haris: I was trained as an upholsterer, but nobody needs that kind of work anymore. Anyway, upholstery was a back-up occupation for me. I wanted to be a rock musician. I played in bars as a vocalist. Without the war, if we'd gone on with that tempo, we'd have made it. I recorded even during the war two songs dedicated to the army.

I wrote the lyrics.

J.N.: You play in weddings?
Haris: No. All weddings are alike. Let it thunder and burn. That's what they want. People listen to Serb music here. You got to play no matter what, even in Muslim weddings, but someone in the audience might hate the music and shoot you. In Serb weddings, someone might ask for you to play Muslim music. It really doesn't matter whether you are a Serb or a Muslim. Anybody can go crazy and shoot you. Sometimes I play for the U.N. parties, but they think we are all cattle here, so they pay us five German marks, enough for hay.

J.N.: Has the war changed the music here?
Haris: Music hasn't changed because of the war. When there was no bombing, people would get together and play music, that is, when there was electricity. Don't you know, we invented unplugged music? We unplugged rock. Clapton and Sting stole it from us. We've got to sue them. (Haris laughs.)

J.N.: Some people believe that the war was caused by religious divisions.
Haris: Nonsense. If people were religious, they wouldn't have to kill each other. When you have Orthodox priests feeding the artillery pieces to blow up civilians, you can't say they are priests. It's not Orthodoxy that caused anything; more likely the lack of it.

J.N.: Does religion affect your social life?
Haris: What religion? You saw the mini-skirts. More than in New York, I believe. There are enough women here—more than men— even for export. But they are picky.

J.N. Where are your parents?
Haris: I no longer talk to Father. He's somewhere abroad. He left the family before the war. I don't need to talk to him. My mother

died from a heart attack a couple of years ago. Too much stress, probably. She had gone to France, where my eighteen-year-old brother had a surgery. His calf muscles were cut and the surgeons reconnected his nerves and arteries. Surgery succeeded, but not fully.

J.N.: Do you want to leave Sarajevo?
Haris: Why would I go to the States, for example? There are thousands of bands better than ours; I don't want to embarrass myself. But I would go there to record. There are good professionals there. There are recording companies in Sarajevo, but you have to pay for the recording, you need contacts to make it, even in music. If you are a member of a party...

J.N.: Why don't you join a party?
Haris: How long will the party last? You could find me in a ditch with a knife in my chest a month later. It used to be safer before the war; the police were strong. Thank God for the cops.

J.N.: So how do you make a living?
Haris: Odd jobs. Slave labor. It doesn't matter. Ditches, construction, music. I work a lot because I have to take care of my brother, not just financially. He adores me. So if he's to imitate me, let him learn how to work like me.

J.N.: How have you changed because of the war?
Haris: I lost many close friends in the war. Nobody can sell tall tales to me any more. I got smarter, and I feel like I am forty-five.

J.N.: What are the best memories from your childhood?
Haris (laughs): Childhood? (Gets serious.) All of them, good and bad, before the war. I can't isolate one or two; they are all together. Every memory before the war is dear to me.

After I turned off the tape recorder, Haris talked enthusiastically, with several gloomy moments, about his experiences at the front. He didn't want me to put them down on paper. Haris said that if his nerves were good enough, he'd write a gigantic novel about the war.

Bojana, 25. Serb.

JN: Did you stay in Sarajevo during the war?

Bojana: I lived in Sarajevo since early childhood. I left in July '92 because of the war. I thought I would come back in a couple of months. These four years I have lived in Pristina, in Kosovo, as a student. I still want to get my law degree, but during the war, I lost self-confidence. I don't know how to study any more, and I worry about money and people. I don't see any future for me here. I'd like to live abroad not because I believe that it would be much better there, but out of principle. If I can't live in my hometown, I might just as well live abroad, where at least the economy functions.

JN: What was the best thing about Sarajevo before the war?

Bojana: Friendships here were the best in the world. To be a friend meant as much as being a brother or sister. But now it's different. Maybe we were divided even before, but you couldn't feel it. Now the divisions are oppressive. We don't even speak the same language. I used to love Muslims. I used to say *kafa* as most people called coffee here, and now I can't say *kahva*, the new Bosnian Muslim way. And in a Croatian town outside Sarajevo, I have to say *kava*. That's unpleasant.

JN: Can't you live in Pristina?

Bojana: In Pristina, with the ninety-five percent Albanian majority, there are no prospects for me as a Serb. It's a Serb police state, artificial, precarious. You can't have friends with Albanians, only with Serbs. They have their cafés, we have ours. You can't even meet them really.

JN: Where would you like to live?

Bojana: I wouldn't like to live in Serbia or Yugoslavia. Even in Serbia, though I am a Serb, I am a visitor. America. Maybe "Beverly Hills" has formed my image of the country; I'm sure it's quite different from what I imagine. But you can probably work your way up there. I would at first have to wash dishes, clean apartments, do demeaning work. But I have the energy. And maybe, if the truth be told, I wouldn't dream of all these places if I wasn't about to be thrown out of the student housing. My term is up. Otherwise I could live there for a decade.

JN: How did the war change you?

Bojana: I'm only twenty-five, but I feel like I'm forty. I wish I had gone abroad five years ago because now I could help my mother. If I went to the States, I would like to take along a lot of people. Even the doorman in the student housing and the cleaning ladies. I don't even know whether I can even leave Pristina. I am emotional, and I form ties. Of course, I couldn't bring them along, but ideally, in my head, I would.

JN: Although you are a Serb, you seem to be more comfortable in Bosnia than in Serbia. Is there such a thing as a Bosnian identity?

Bojana: I think there is such a thing as a Bosnian identity. All of us from Bosnia—Serbs, Muslims, and Croats—have more in common with each other than let's say Serbs from Serbia and Serbs from Bosnia. So there should be a Bosnian nation, not just Muslim, but a nation that includes all of us from Bosnia. The divisions into enclaves and cantons is contrary to the nature of what I understand as Bosnia. I would like to live in a united Bosnia, but if Bosnia is going to be a bunch of fragments, I am definitely out of here.

Lila Mulic, 28. Muslim.

Lila didn't need any questions. After she'd heard me interview Bojana, she was ready for her story.

My father is a Muslim, my mother a Croat, so I count as a Muslim. Before the war I had a boyfriend, a house, a job, and I was happy. But my lover, who was a Muslim, was killed. That haunts me. His parents were thrown out of their apartment. We go to the graveyard together. I'm also helping my parents. My mother is sick, unemployed, retired.

I'm looking for a partner, so I could have children, to look forward rather than to just think about the past. I'm a Scorpio. Many people don't believe in astrology, but I do. You know, it's hard for a Scorpio to live alone.

Still it's not easy. I have to live on three hundred Deutsche marks a month.

I'm twenty-eight, and I still believe in love but in love where there's no sub-text. Now, when there's a shortage of apartments, people could be with you simply because they want a decent place to live.

War didn't change me. Before the war I had more non-Muslim friends. I don't want to die for hunger because I am a Muslim. I think the war made me stronger. If I went through it, I should be able to go through anything.

I am no more religious now than before. I go to the mosque now and then. But I admit it, I haven't read the Koran except for a page here and there. But I worship at the gravestone of my boyfriend. That's my shrine.

I love to write a line, my own, or to copy in calligraphy from my favorite books. For example, from *The Bridge on the Drina* by Ivo Andric: "Forgetting cures everything. Suffering is the best kind of forgetting because in suffering we remember only what we love." Or, how about this? "I would like to sit by the river to throw my past into the waters so it could never come back. Then I could sing until the daybreak."

Berislav Matijevic, 28. Croat.
JN: How was it to stay here during the war?
Berislav: In the beginning of the war, it was terrible, but later I got

used to it, so although I was afraid, I could live almost normally. Once when I was asleep, a projectile flew though the window, penetrated my floor and exploded in the apartment below. So I could have easily died then.

JN: What's your occupation?
Berislav: I'm a machine technician by training. I couldn't find work before the war, and I can't find it now. So in that sense, nothing changed. The economy was just as bad here before except that Volkswagen Golf used to be made here.

JN: How do you spend your time?
Berislav: I listen to Moody Blues. I read Rudolf Steiner. Anthroposophy. And I discuss things with this philosopher here. (He nudges Vadim jovially.)

JN: You are good friends, although you come from different ethnic backgrounds?
Berislav: People don't trust each other these days because of ethnic divisions. But the two of us were never interested in that. There are people who can't make friends in other national groups—well, that's their right. Our right is to get along as well.

JN: Would you like to go to the West? And if you went, what kind of work would you like to get?
Berislav: I would like some kind of conveyor belt job so I can think freely. I don't care if they enslave my body, but I want my mind to be free for philosophy.

JN: How come you are not married?
Berislav: When I meet women, I start to philosophize and they run away from me. I told one woman that death was a pretty good thing as a transition to a spiritual existence and that spiritual existence was superior to the physical. She said, I want to live! She thought I wanted a suicide pact with her. She fled. I never saw her again.

Anyway, I'm free. That's what matters to me. I was free before, I'm free now.

Vadim, 30 years old.

JN: What's your ethnic background?

Vadim: I'm a Muslim by birth, but I feel that I'm a Buddhist. So if you ask me what nationality I am, I'll tell you I'm a Buddhist.

JN: What was your occupation before the war?

Vadim: I worked as a film projectionist, showing movies in various theaters around the city. And in my free time, I read a lot. We always sought spiritual things. I started with Carlos Castaneda.

Communists brought all that crap here. Rather than that we should study computers and become practical and Westernized, they pushed fancy books—Taoism, Zen—and I read that and lost touch with reality. Serbs wanted us to be impractical. The Belgrade literature was all like that, whatever they brought to us. I guess, if religion is the opiate of the masses, they brought us literature of all sorts of religions, except they didn't want us to practice our own. You couldn't really be a zealous Muslim or a practicing Christian, but something zany was all right with them.

JN: Do you two know each other for a long time?

Vadim: We are friends from the peace time. We got to know each other after a lecture on alternative medicine, about bioenergy. There were all sorts of people here who pretended to have special powers, who knew all the grasses that could heal you, who could bend nails with their eyes. People wanted to believe anything.

JN: How about you? Did you practice any religion?

Vadim: I was a Hari Krishna. Now and then I still visit the group. Because of that, the government made a dossier about me that I was crazy, which turned out to my advantage: I didn't have to fight in the army in the first six months. But the law suddenly changed and I was drafted. Anyway, crazy or not, I wouldn't like to be a Hari

Krishna anymore. That's too Far East for me. I'm interested in meditation, but in a modern way.

During the war, I reread Carlos Castaneda. We meditated but took no drugs. Before the war, I was a vegetarian. I didn't eat eggs, drink milk.

JN: Would you like to leave Sarajevo? What country would you go to?

Vadim: Europe. Europe is one country to us. Austria. France. I've never been abroad, but from pictures and literature I have a good understanding of what it's like there. I like countries where there's a discipline, work, where people work and think as individuals. Here, we all think collectively. That's what's destroyed us. One national group blaming another, instead of everyone taking care of his own business. I don't think we know how to be alone. See, many of your questions you address to me, and I answer in the plural, with "we." Our egos are crushed. What else do I like about Europe? Parks. See, there are no trees here. People had to burn them down for heat. See there are a couple of bushes there, there was some kind of reforestation program; but we'll be old men before trees can shade us again in the summer. Anyway, it's hard to go to the West. Germans don't accept refugees any more. So it would be better if the West came here. But I don't think anybody is investing.

JN: What kind of work would you do abroad?

Vadim: I would like to work with electronics. I've been trained to work with electronic equipment. In Germany, I have two uncles, but neither of them said, "Come here, be with us for awhile."

J.N.: So, you praised individualism. They are practicing it. It could have a downside: everybody can ignore everybody.

Vadim: That's all right with me. Better than what we have.

JN: So if you can't go abroad, what's the prospect here?

Vadim: We are used to waiting. We are all waiting. The West is waiting, we are waiting, and years are passing. I think that the West has some interests here. They know what they want here. I don't want to talk about that. That's their thing. But this time I don't want dreams. Communists have sold us too many dreams for too long. I'd like to see some serious enterprise around here. Enough religion. I want economics. I'll be the first to work.

The following evening in Zagreb, the national teams of Bosnia & Herzegovina and Croatia were playing a qualifying soccer match for the world championship. We went to a café in the walking zone in Bascarsija, near the largest mosque, where the match was televised. Near our table sat a group of five young men. Their cheering, as any cheering in sports, was one-sided, for the Bosnian team. The Croatian goal keeper made a ridiculous error. An easy ball that a defensive player of Croatia passed on to him, and our neighbors stood up and shrieked, "There, you Croatian monkeys!"

Later, a Croatian player scored with a long-distance shot. "How could this happen? They didn't even have the opportunity?" The neighbors wailed and swore. Then when the Bosnian team attacked, the neighbors commented, "Just shoot at the goal keeper; he's got water in his head. You'll score." A man commented that he wouldn't trust the goalie with keeping his chickens.

The Croatian team scored again, from up close, after several passes, and now led two to one. The neighbors were freaking out. "Oh, how I hate these Croats. Anybody but them. If we could at least take away a point from them in Zagreb so they couldn't go to the world championship. I hate them."

I didn't feel comfortable cheering for the Croatian team next to them so I did it in English. Even so, I wondered when the tables could be turned, literally... This reminded me of a joke. A man came back from Germany to Croatia and said to a friend of his, "Man, they have real democracy there. You can say anything you like and nobody will jail you for that." The friend replied, "Here too, in German you can say anything you like."

The Balkan wars started basically in a *1990* Zagreb match

between Dinamo (Zagreb) and Red Star (Belgrade), when Croatian fans jumped onto the field after a referee had apparently favored the Serb team. The Serb-run army came to help the police, most enthusiastically. Zvonimir Boban, a Croatian who played for Milan, hit a policeman to defend a fan. The match was suspended, but the match escalated the nationalist conflict between Croats and Serbs. People kept protesting in the streets against Serbian police and army. According to many soccer fans, the Balkan wars started as soccer wars, and the only way to make peace again was to expand the league so Serbs, Muslims, and Croats could play soccer together again.

Just as we were ending our visit before the September 14 elections, a bomb exploded in front of the Croatian Democratic Union headquarters in Sarajevo. We visited the housing under-secretary in Sarajevo, Zlatko Horvat, one of only two Croats working in the ministry, according to him. He claimed that the fate of Bosnia lay in the distribution of houses and apartments: it was basically a real-estate issue. Recently a law was introduced to allow the refugees who stayed in vacated apartments to live there until they found better arrangements. Now, what that meant in Sarajevo was that the Muslim refugees who recently came from Srebrenica and many other places could stay in the apartments previously owned by Serbs and Croats for as long as they liked. Sarajevo had become basically a mono-ethnic city, Muslim, in a backlash against Serbian ethnic cleansing.

Horvat, a trained military officer in the old Yugoslav army, talked to me and smoked a cigarette on a holder made out of ornate wood, something I had seen among the Russians. He showed me thousands of complaints of Croats and Serbs who couldn't move into their old apartments, and then the lists that showed the distribution of international aid for reconstruction of private homes. All the names on the lists were Muslim. He marshalled statistics: in the Muslim-Croat conflict in Bosnia and Herzegovina, *145,000* Croats and *55,000* Muslims were expelled from their homes. Out of the pre-war population of *750,000*, only *300,000* Croats remained in the Republic. "It's for historians to decide who did more ethnic cleansing," he said. "I show only facts." Croats were declared an aggressor equal to the Serbs, although the Serbs, led by Radovan Karadjic, started the war in Bosnia and in the former Yugoslavia after Slobadan Milosevic abolished the autonomous status of Vojvodina and Kosovo. Horvat said, "Sarajevo as the capital of the federation cannot be constituted of one ethnic group. Otherwise, it's a federation among whom?"

Anyway, Croats had and have legitimate complaints. Muslims do too, for Croats and Serbs can unite against them.

Jon and I looked forward to driving out of Sarajevo. We had grown weary of destroyed buildings, I of translating conversations and he of being isolated linguistically. Even north of Sarajevo, we drove through destroyed villages, accumulating oppressive impressions. What to do with the impressions? To simply feel a bit sentimental and say a platitude, "Isn't this terrible? So sad!" Well, everybody knows that it must be sad. To write our impressions from the trip through former war zones, superficially, as observers? Only a participant, someone burnt out of his hearth, could give you the tragedy of what had happened there deeply and legitimately enough. I could agree with Sára Karig that travelogues were pretty much futile.

Before driving through the Serb corridor, I had to get rid of the materials I had gotten in the foreign journalists' office in Croatia, where the press director had given me several books on atrocities committed by Serbs. I had already thrown out the books on atrocities committed by Muslims before entering Bosnia and Herzegovina, lists of names of people who were killed. In case there was a checkpoint in the Serb Republic, this might not be healthy literature to show. Before the border, in a curve—of which there was no shortage—I threw away the literature. Otherwise, driving through the Serb corridor near Brcko was no problem, even though there had recently been violent incidents between Serbs and the international forces around there. No checkpoints. Serbs deliberately kept a low profile along the main road.

In Orasje on the river Sava, we waited for more than two hours for the ferry that took cars to Croatia, close to the old destroyed bridge. There was a new bridge being built, but it stretched only halfway from Croatia toward Bosnia. Then, once again, we were on the Highway of Brotherhood and Unity, experiencing the deceptive sensation of freedom moving 140 kilometers an hour provides.

A PLACE IN BETWEEN

During my stay in Croatia in *1997*, I drove through a village, Medjuric, where neither I nor any of my ancestors were born but where some of them had lived for a good while: two decades or so, and a grandfather, for five.

I didn't plan merely to drive through, though Medjuric means "a place in between," on my way to Zagreb. I wanted to stop by and visit my mother's brother for half an hour of so, provided I could find him quickly. Danko had lived here from infancy till manhood, almost. When he was sixteen, the war broke out and Ustasha soldiers marched in, and they would have merely marched by hadn't Danko laughed at how short the captain was. The captain was short but his hearing was sharp and long, and he came over to the tall youth and drafted him. Danko fled from the Ustasha barracks in Zagreb and became a partisan, not for any communist or liberation ideology, but because he feared that Ustashas would shoot him if they found him again in Zagreb or Medjuric.

I had asked my mother, in Daruvar forty kilometers north, for his address. She said nobody there went by addresses, that just as you go over the top of the hill, the second or third house on the right must be his. Well, I went over a hill and another, past a wooden house where I thought I had visited for a funeral a long time ago.

I stepped out of the car in the drizzly mist. Behind a fence of gray and bending planks of wood stood a peasant in blue worker's clothes, light from washing; he had a couple of teeth in his jaws, behind his thin lips. As I stood out of the rented car, he said, "You are a Bubanovic? Or a Novakovic." He asked even before I had the time to ask anything.

"Yes, I am both," I said. "How did you know?"

Just one look at me sufficed for him to see my maternal and my paternal lines.

"Faces are faces," he said. "It's easy to put them together. And you are looking for Danko?"

"Yes, how did you know?"

"I didn't. But why wouldn't you look for him? Who else do you have here?"

"Nobody. Where is his house?"

"Drive down one kilometer. And when you see"—and here he used one word that I didn't know but thought to mean a heap of gravel—"he's on the other side of the road, just there."

I was, for no reason I could think of, embarrassed to admit that I didn't know that word. The sound of many consonants seemed to me like a heap of gravel, and besides, what else can be on the side of the road? I forgot the sound of the word before the man's sentence ceased to lisp out of his mouth. So how could I say, "What was that word, that you said was on the side of the road?"

I was sure that it was a dialect word, which I should know from my roots, and which my mother would know and my father would know, even if it turned out to be Czech (and there were many Bohemians in the village and we were part Bohemian). While I enjoyed this link, the commonness—that a peasant could know me from five decades ago, though five decades ago I didn't exist. But my lines did, and he knew those lines and strung them together like a fisherman and caught my image in the net. I didn't want to dwell on one word, a simple word, that could destroy the commonness.

I asked the peasant what his last name was, and he said, "Novosel." We were not related but our names were similar; they started the same way. He laughed at recognitions, cordially; he stepped from one foot to another, quickly, and back, as if dancing; this easy encounter made his morning and mine.

I thought, this is good, good enough. I don't need to visit anybody; the village where I am not from has much of me without my doing anything about it whatsoever. What should I add to this and what should I take away? The moment was perfect, easy, done.

Maybe, I thought, my experience would be even better—more of a trip into the past to something resembling a home—if I saw the uncle. Not my not knowing a word but my being embarrassed that I didn't know it broke the bond, not with the peasant nor with something resembling roots but with the uncle.

I thought that even if I couldn't find the house there would be other peasants around and about. But I ran into nobody else. The mist lifted from the street, and there was only one long street, and I could see far. I passed a bundle of thick wires that sagged low and climbed into sharp wave-tips from a nearby power plant, passed diesel-besotted railroad tracks with my grandfather's gravestone only several yards from the tracks. On the road shortly afterward, I did see a heap of gravel, but on the other side of the road not one but two quiet houses, their curtains drawn, their yards and fowl still. I got out of the car, thought of walking into a yard, knocking, but I didn't do it. If the uncle came out of the yard now, if it turned out easy, fine.

Maybe I would drive through again, but now I had to reach Zagreb. And so I didn't see Danko. His son and daughter-in-law, too, now lived here. The son had loved doves since his boyhood. He'd had doves that could fly out of Zagreb to the village and back, he claimed. But the family left Zagreb with his retired father and never went back. Maybe the doves did. I could ask all that, even see the thirtieth generation of doves, who knows. I drove on and thought of what my mother said of Danko.

It would be hard to understand Danko because he slurred his words through overuse of alcohol, and he lisped them because he had lost his dentures. He covered his mouth because he was embarrassed that he didn't have anything resembling teeth in it. He lost the dentures while teaching his grandson to swim in a fish-farm. He got to the middle of the lake, laughing and chuckling for joy, for the grandson could now swim with him, and in a good snort of chuckling and water, the dentures he had got a while back in the Federative Republic of Yugoslavia sailed out and sank and zigzagged to the fertilized bottom. He dived, and his son dived later; pretty soon three generations dived, but they couldn't find the dentures in the muddy bottom. Danko couldn't afford new dentures at seven hundred German marks, yet he didn't miss socialized medicine, which perhaps ruined his teeth to begin with. My mother said, "He'll keep talking anyway, but you probably won't understand much of what he says. Even in the best of shape, with the dentures in and the alcohol out of his head, it would be hard to follow his rusty trains of thought. But do visit him. He would love it, and he will be upset if he finds out that you were there and didn't visit him."

Well, I was in Medjuric, and I merely passed by. Unless the old man with two teeth in his jaws was my uncle. But of course, that wasn't him. My uncle is Bubanovic, not Novosel.

I drove from the village past many brown hawks on fence posts. That morning the hawks were lazy; they fluffed up their wings and sank their necks into the feathers to keep the drizzle away. None of them flew at the quarries within my sight. I went onto a highway ramp. The mists came and went in wisps on the highway of Brotherhood and Unity, whose name had been changed to something else, perhaps Freedom. I am not sure; I don't remember the new name. I'd slur it anyway, into a foreign tongue, and that wouldn't add anything.

This could mark the end of the anti-story, and for a while it did. I wrote it last year. This year, I was in Croatia again, with a friend, in a rented car, and we were in a rush to go to Zagreb. It occurred to me that I could change the route from Daruvar and go through Medjuric.

This time, I found Danko. I knocked on his low, two-windowed house's door. First I couldn't hear his, "Yes, come in," because there was a goose honking at the same time. I knocked again, and now I heard the voice say to come in. I did. It was dark inside, and a man in his pajamas, prisoner-style, striped and blue, stood there. I said, "Hi, Uncle. This is me, Josip."

"So what?" he said.

What now? He was confused and didn't recognize me. I said again my name, "Josip, Josipov (son of Josip), son of Ruth (his sister)."

"Ah, so!" he exclaimed. We shook hands. His was heavy and it shook. He still hadn't got the upper teeth, but they were not all gone. His eyes had a cataract in them. There was a scar on his head. We sat on a bench in his yard.

"My wife is in the field, and when she comes back, she'll give you something to eat and drink."

"Don't worry. Just passing through, for ten minutes, to see you," I said.

"I am not well. My eyes are failing, there's a buzz in my ears, and I am dizzy. That's all I can say. I am not complaining, I'm seventy-four, and for two wars and two jail terms, that's pretty good.

"And look at our country. Here in Balkans we can't do anything without wars. Not like the Czechs and Slovaks. They know how to get along even if they hate each other. Here, our Serbs went beserk, tore up the country. They don't even worry about the fact that I protected them as a partisan from the beginning of the war. I was wounded twice. What can you do?"

As we sat outside, a goat appeared in the window of a barrack in his yard, a beautiful white goat, and stared at us. I wished I had more time to talk with my uncle, but my friend couldn't keep sitting in the car and waiting, and so I shook hands again and said good-bye to him.

He stood at his metal gate, shaking, his eyes hazy, his hair white, with several shocks and cowlicks, uncombed, not quite shaven nor unshaven, and he struck me as terribly sad, human, honest. He kept talking about the awful state of affairs here, low retirement payments. He couldn't smile, maybe his muscles wouldn't allow it. I remembered how he used to smile, with his cheeks shiny and ruddy and one gold-capped tooth glittering from his mouth. But he was always soft-spoken, shy to some extent. Anyway, talking to him, sensing his nearness to death, and my inability to help, I was filled with remorse that I hadn't tried harder to visit him earlier, when he was fresher, or to create time now. Of course, who visits relatives anymore?

WRITING HOME

HVAR

The Dalmatian coast of Croatia resembles a Dalmatian dog's back, the dots representing islands—nearly a thousand islands. The islands have an intoxicating and mysterious end-of-the world quality about them.

According to a few scholars, this is where Odysseus was lost for years—the names of two Dalmatian islands, Krk and Korcula, may be cognates of the enchantress Kirke (Circe). At least the consonants match. The story may or may not, but once you are here, you do feel like getting lost in the beauty.

While the islands are provinces of a provincial country, there are surprising moments of history on every island, and especially Hvar. Stari Grad, a town on the island of Hvar, stems from a Greek polis, Pharos, founded in 324 B.C.. The town of Hvar used to be the main Venetian naval outpost in the Eastern Adriatic and as such was prosperous.

Peasant and commoner revolts against the nobles were frequent, and the one in 1510 might have been successful for a few years had it not been debilitated by peasants having visions of the bleeding cross and resorting to a massive self-flagellation, which went on for weeks and allowed the nobles to escape and to regroup. The Turkish navy smashed Hvar in 1571 and just as the town was rebuilt in 1579, lightning hit its castle's huge storage of gunpowder; the resulting explosion wiped most houses off the slope. Battles were so common here that the town theater—the oldest extant indoor theater in Europe—bears the inscription, *Built in the Second Year of Peace, 1612.* Despite the destruction, the town has arisen many times, and now it displays an architectural unity: no high-rises mar the lines the houses of gray and white stone make, with cobbled streets made out of the marble from the island of Brac.

I came to Hvar as an accidental tourist, accompanying my eight-year-old son, Joseph, who enrolled as a cello student in the splendid summer music school, Uzmah (Upbeat), in the town of Hvar. The school has some of the best music teachers from all over the world. My wife, Jeanette, and my daughter Eva, who was four, joined us, ready to swim and play. We bought a used ten-year-old Rover in Zagreb; there were many cheap cars offered in the newspapers, and buying a used car seemed a better way to go than to rent, although for a shorter stay, renting would be easier. We drove from Zagreb to Split through the rugged terrain of the former Krajina, and from Split we took a ferry to Hvar. Through tourist agencies and acquaintances, we got leads on apartments to rent, and on the edge of the town, near the water front, we rented a two-room, two double-bed apartment, with a kitchenette, a terrace with a view of several small islands in the distance, and a decent-sized bathroom. A little park of cypress and pine trees separated the apartment from the promenade along the bay.

Nearly every evening, my family and I took walks along the shore to the central piazza and the marina in the town of Hvar. We marveled at the intensity of the blues of the sky and the sea and the greens of the cypresses. Many people in Croatia claim that the farther south in the Adriatic you go, the more beautiful the islands become; Hvar is one of the southernmost islands, the fifth in size, about fifty miles long and ranging from two to four miles wide. Especially the western part of the island where the town of Hvar is located is one of the sunniest spots in Europe, with 1,722 sunny hours a year, and for that reason, as well as the relative purity of the sea and the unity of style of the old Venetian architecture, the town is one of the prime elite resorts in Croatia. Only 4,000 people live year-round in the town; in Croatia the town inhabitants are famous for their friendliness and joviality; all the sunshine apparently does improve one's moods. Other than tourism, fishing, and wine-making, there's little economy here, and people move at a slow, leisurely pace, as though they have no worry in the world. With plenty of fresh produce in the town market, the plentiful daily catch of fish, and the habit of drinking red wine with water (*bevanda*) and strolling, the people here seem very healthy.

In the evening groups of old men, and sometimes of old women, gather near the sea, and sing, in what is known as *Dalmatinska Klapa*, polyphonous songs about the beauty of the sea, old loves, youth. The cheerful atmosphere of this town of white stone and palms attracts many connoiseurs. During our stay, Goran Ivanisevic, the Wimbledon champion, docked in the town marina, right near the center. Several British royal family members had visited the town a few months before, and the largest luxury liner in the world, *Wind Surf*, docked for a week half a mile outside the town. The current Croatian and Slovenian presidents relaxed in their summer homes here. The glamour of the place is obvious to so many people that the town grew crowded in mid-August, and therefore my family and I looked for beauty away from the shore (and other marvelous shore resort towns here, such as Jelsa, Vrboska, Stari Grad), in the inland parts of Hvar.

Ten kilometers from Hvar, we visited an old ghost hamlet, Zarace, inlaid into a steep slope over the ever-changing shades of the sea. The air was fragrant with herbs, pines, and salty winds. We climbed the stone paths; the stone houses seemed to be an extension of the piled rock fences that prevented soil erosion. Hvar inhabitants claim the island used to be a lush forest and rich fields, but two forces stripped much of it down to the rocky bone: goats, which overgrazed it, and Venetians, who mercilessly logged it, like most of the eastern Adriatic. In Zarace one house looked nicely kept, its doors wide and open, and two tables sat outside under an arch of grapes, with wine glasses next to barrels and old dried wine-skins.

We found the host, Pero, the only inhabitant of the hamlet, stoking the fire in the open space of a former wine cellar, *konoba*. His hearth, which served mostly him and his friends, occasionally worked as a restaurant, provided you first gave him a call on his cell phone (which we did) several hours in advance for fish, and a day in advance for lamb.

Pero brought out his homemade red wine and a mixed salad made from his garden's yield: tomatoes, cucumbers, parsley. He told us the hamlet used to be completely abandoned. An Englishman wanted to buy it to turn it into an art colony, but several home-owners refused to sell even though they lived in Hvar and had no use for these houses. Pero thought other people might move in, but he was in no rush to welcome them. I could see what he meant as we watched in quietude the last sunrays lick the sea, then the island's tip.

Another evening, we were charmed by Vrisnik, a hamlet, which got its name from aromatic heather. The whole hamlet smelled of rosemary. At the entrance to the town we met a man who rode a white mule, sitting sideways. An old woman was fixing the stone fence of her tomato patch. Streets zigzagged down the slope through low arches. Many houses tilted, with sagging doors, cracked wooden frames, and unpainted windows; there was a forsaken beauty here. The streets looked as they may have two hundred years ago, except older, decrepit, on the edge between ruins of history and glimmers of the future. Time has stopped here, but another dawn is on the horizon, refracting through cold beer foam on the tourists' tables.

At the bottom of the town, we found a restaurant, Konoba Vrisnik. The owner, who was both cook and waiter, told us that he'd been a chef at a hotel in Hvar, but when the war came, the hotel closed down, and there was nothing for him to do. So he built the addition to his house for the restaurant, using antique mill treads for beams. He prepared a delicious meal for us: three pounds of garlicky bluefish, served with his homemade wine.

After a few of these excursions, we relaxed at our temporary home. We swam in the amazingly transparent azure waters right outside of our apartment. My son learned how to use flippers and to snorkel. From the beach, we watched at the passenger ships go by. Once a week we took a trip in the small boat which left from the Hvar Marina to Pakleni Otoci archipelago, only a kilometer away from Hvar, and we stayed at St. Clement Island, the biggest one in the Pakleni chain. This is where an officer of Napoleon's army, Juraj Toto Meneghello, retired (Napoleon, of course, ended up on an island as well) because of the beauty of the place, and his descendents still own much of the island. My kids were wild about the Palmizana beach, because it is sandy and shallow and lined with caves where you can shun the sun and play hide and seek. For dinner, we walked up the hill through a palm grove to Meneghello Place Restaurant, which hosts an art gallery and Sunday recitals. After listening to Bartok's *Mosquito Dance* performed by two violinists, one from the Berlin Philharmonic and another from the Bolshoi Theater Orchestra, I ate a splendid seabass, even the liver and the adrenal glands, which I imagined gave me a special rush. While I rummaged through the organs and rolled them and melted them over my tongue, I bowed in stealthy pleasure, under the impression that the guests at the restaurant avoided looking at my obscene hedonism. Eva, my four-year old, asked me whether I had found the soul of the fish and what it tasted like and whether it had become a ghost in my throat.

"No, dear, we did not go quite that far," I replied.

THIN AND FAT CATS

"Oh, you've plumped up." A man I hadn't seen in three years laughed and patted my belly. That was the first sentence I heard in Croatia upon my coming back for a visit. "Oh, we are looking prosperous, aren't we?" said another friend, and stroked my belly. After a while, I found this form of greeting quite irritating, and despite the jovial tone in which it was conducted, I imagined there was a lot of meanness disguised underneath it. *You may live in the States, you may have a better car than I do, but, look at you, you are basically a pig.*

It is easy to be thin here. People walk all over the city. Even if they drive, parking is so difficult (there are no multi-story parking ramps), that they end up walking. Offices are scattered all around the city. If you want to accomplish anything, you end up running, and since hardly anybody has money, you don't sit down for a meal in a restaurant. In the morning, people rarely have eggs, but simply a slice of bread and a slice of some kind of disgusting sausage, after a bite of which one grimaces and walks out. You might get a news-paper on the way, read about war criminals and massive embezzle-ments by government officials. You drink espresso made of the cheapest grain of coffee, which will make you grimace even more. Whatever enclosed space you enter will be basically a cloud of cheap tobacco, whose purpose—at least it seems so to me—is to intensify the nausea and lessen any potential appetite. Now you'll be sure not to eat for most of the day, and in the evening, depressed, you may get drunk and forget about eating, and on national holidays, you'll eat half a suckling pig. So it doesn't look like a healthy thinness but is thinness nevertheless. And with us Americans, it's never-the-less, or as Oscar Wilde put it, "Bulk is the American canon of beauty." Of course, bulk no longer is the American canon of beauty when it comes to bodies, but we are certainly used to it, and other than in the media, mostly relaxed about it.

It's hard to get used to walking around as a fat American cat abroad. Our American national self-image, of course, is a bit more flattering when we are abroad, so in a group of Americans on the way to St. Petersburg, Russia, for a conference, people were joking about Russian *babushkas*. They expected Russians to be fat. My American compatriots were amazed, however, when we took a walk on Nevsky Prospekt, to elbow their way through droves of tall, thin women who paraded nearly naked, in mini-skirts. Now, this too was not a healthy thin: many of the women looked gaunt, a bit blue in the face, perhaps heroin thin. Salaries in Russia are so low that people sometimes choose to starve if they want to save money for anything. I thought the thinness was pretty much spontaneous, but a Russian friend of mine explained to me that it was a studied thinness: many young women read fashion columns, look at pictures of the models, and deliberately starve. It's mostly poverty thinness, turned into a semblance of glamour. And ours is a prosperity fatness turned into slovenliness.

Worrying about the body image is certainly a superficial and demeaning business, but the consolation in my travels is this: we in America aren't alone in the superficiality. Europeans may have surpassed us.

LETTER FROM CROATIA

Larry, you surprised me, asking for something so antique as a "Letter from Croatia" rather than a formal essay, but the idea of setting down my observations in epistolary form thrilled me. Twenty-five years ago, upon emigrating, I fell in love with writing while composing very long letters, mostly to my friends in Croatia, from the States. Writing to them as persons, not as a faceless readership, gave me a chance to see and hear and feel what I was experiencing both from their perspective and mine; I could synthesize the new and the old perceptions of this incessantly surprising country. But the main thing was the pleasure of retelling strange things, letter to letter, depending on the unique background and personality of my reader. Since my friends still had one another for long conversations, they did not write much to me, but I kept writing out of habit, and soon, instead of letters which failed to simulate the dialogue I wanted, I began to shape stories and essays to recreate the original pleasure I took in long letter-writing.

I have been going back to Croatia on and off for almost a year, and other than a few e-mails I haven't written a single letter. Although you asked me to write for the readers of *Michigan Quarterly Review*, it's best that I address you since I can't envision writing a communal letter. Of course I expect your readers to eavesdrop, as we all like to do in public places, especially when matters like travel and politics are being discussed. One virtue of letters, or let's say one illusion of letters, is that they don't strain visibly for the *mot juste*, nor do they need to be carefully revised like stories and essays They can be a bit raw, like a conversation. So, here goes...

My family and I came here last May when I got some time off from teaching. We planned to spend a year in Europe, and, if we liked the change of scene, we would simply move. Having lived in polluted and conservative Cincinnati, spending too much time in traffic and wading through shopping malls, we longed for an alternative, a saner life, pedestrian style, and so we booked passage to Zagreb. We would have preferred Greece or France or some other glamorously healthy country, but because of my roots in Croatia, and my need for new materials for my work, this stretch of the Balkans made the most sense. Besides, my mother, who still lives in my hometown, seemed to be near death, and we wanted our children to spend some time with her. They would learn another language, get cheap music lessons, and see the world from a different perspective than the American super-power one. Croatia is an infra-power, or hypopower. The world looks a lot more threatening and complicated from down here than from the U.S.

We enrolled Joseph, seven, and Eva, three, in the local elementary school and preschool, respectively. That introduced us to how things functioned here. Everybody told us that Croatian schools were hard, kids were under a lot of pressure to learn, etc. However, instead of starting on the fourth of September—already late by our American standards—the opening was postponed at the end of August because of the heat wave unil the eleventh. And though the first week of September was unusually cool, the heat wave delay stayed in effect. And later, under every imaginable pretext, classes were canceled and new holidays introduced. I thought absenteeism was something kids contrived, not teachers and administrators, but I learned otherwise.

Nearly all the people we talked to in Zagreb complained about

the rushed tempo of modern life and the unrelenting work sched-
ules, but the evidence was to the contrary. People mostly sat in cafés
near every street corner, drank foul coffee with loads of sugar or
half-liter beers, and talked on cell phones. Everyone here loves to
stay away from home and the workplace, so the most reliable way to
get in touch with them is via cell phones, which, despite their supposed poverty, nearly everybody owns. I felt almost proud of
Americans, who seem to have resisted the cell culture, unlike the
Europeans. For a while, we refused to buy a cell phone, much to our
friends' and family's annoyance. "We can't get in touch with you,"
they complained. "Yes, you can, we have a phone." To them, calling
a line phone seems nearly as odd as our sending handwritten letters
on engraved stationery for personal communication.

Even my publishers spend most of their time in coffee shops and
complain to every passerby how overworked they are, how many
manuscripts they read, how not enough people read books. Well,
how can they read if they spend so much time talking? Here, I wit-
nessed a different system of getting published. In the States you
rely on the post office to get your materials to publishers, via an
agent or not, but in Croatia writers go to the hangouts where the
editors and publishers have coffee and talk about the sorry state of
current letters (i.e., profits). The task of a would-be writer is to be
as entertaining as possible, a boon companion, so he or she dresses
well and tells jokes, and following some especially charming inter-
lude slips the manuscript across the table. "I hate it when people
just send me the manuscripts," my publisher told me, "I have too
many. I like to know the authors personally." Of course, it's mainly
assistant editors who actually read these large tomes, or supposedly
do.

Somehow books get published, many of them, but then they
don't get distributed because publishing them was so exhausting the
editors lose interest. Managers of bookstores often forget to pay
the publishers for the books that miraculously do get sold, and to
punish the bookstores, publishers no longer offer their books to
them. And so each publisher has only a few bookstores to sell the

books. A book review comes out, and the reader has to visit a dozen bookstores to find the one that carries the book. If I sound a little cynical, that is the tone I have acquired listening to how things work, in precisely the same coffee shops where I too had precious manuscripts to hand across the table. I blended right in, except I was not as stylishly dressed, nor did I have a Nokia that went off every five minutes with a wedding march. Oh yes, and I did not smoke, so I could not look as soulfully afflicted as my fellow authors. When I gave up on hanging out with the publishers, when I no longer returned their calls and even canceled a few meetings, then they invited me to give them a new book, provided it did not have too many war stories, and provided it had a lot of diverting Americana in it. Even they have gotten tired of wars. In case you wonder what you get paid if you publish a book here, I won't hide that embarrassing fact: five hundred bucks, not enough to live on for a month.

Jeanette thought of finding a teaching position at the university, but she had not completed her Ph.D. yet, and the salary range here struck us as pitiful, around five hundred dollars a month. She thought she could make more through occasional day-trading, but that proved not to be true because of the continuous slide of U.S. stocks. It was a nice illusion, and kept us dependent on the internet service, which in Croatia as in most European countries turned out to be quite expensive because you pay the local phone calls. Still, financially, staying here and renting a two-bedroom apartment for $220 a month seems reasonable. My family is reluctant to leave Croatia, at least until January 2002, whereas I'm committed to a New York Public Library Fellowship in the fall, and I tremble as I read the high rent ads for Manhattan.

Anyhow, for me this experiment in emigration (from America) will be over in a month. In the States, people often ask, "Is your family still in Croatia?" They mean my brothers, sisters, mother. "Yes," I reply, "and they do not plan to leave." When I say that, people look at me blankly, as though it were news that the whole planet does not scheme to come to America. Actually, my grandfather emigrated from Croatia to the States in the beginning of the last century, and after a dozen years of working in metal factories in Cleveland, he gave up on the American dream and went back to Croatia, a quite common reverse migration. In many villages all over the Balkans, you find people who went to America and came back. I thought the same might happen to me, but for now I have changed my mind.

We live in the city, not in the center but not in the suburbs either, and we get around mostly by tram and on foot. I enjoy walking through old gray streets, gazing at the friezes and busts on the walls and roofs, history staring back at me, much of it ugly, and mostly a history of subjugation, of Croatia's being a colonized part of Austria and Hungary, and then of Yugoslavia as an inferior province. Although the city abuts a mountain with forests, and its industry has been decimated by the recent wars, the air here is not much better than in Cincinnati. But the food may be. We go to the farmer's market, two blocks away, and buy produce from old women. Like anywhere else in Eastern Europe, the city is full of old women and not so many old men. Men here don't live healthily; their addiction to tobacco, alcohol, and wars, plus degraded working conditions in factories, have resulted in a shortened average lifespan. The market is a mixture of imported produce from Spain and Italy and Greece as well as home-raised stuff. Egg yolks are dark orange, and when you fry them you have visions of suns setting over the snowy landscape of albumens.

Of course, it would be simpler to live on a farm in the States and raise our own produce, which perhaps is the next step for us in Pennsylvania, where I have a new job. If I were a commercially successful writer, we could settle in Europe. My family would still like to do that, but I would not. Yes, it is an alternative to the American madness, but Croatian culture is still more madness, to my mind.

It is hard to get used to Croatian surliness, backbiting, and envy. For example, nobody in the literary world has anything good to say about one another, except now and then in the press for the most blatant ingratiating reasons. My book of stories came out here last year and received the Kozarac Award for the year's best prose work by a Slavonian writer. At first I got excellent reviews and was interviewed in all the major papers and on TV, but then a journalist made up the information that I had just been granted a National Endowment for the Arts Fellowship of fifty thousand dollars. (I had gotten it a while back in the amount of twenty thousand.) Since she did not know how the Fellowship worked, the journalist said that the American government was paying me fifty thousnd dollars to write. Immediately after that, a review assailing my book came out, mostly centering on the issue of money. "What would our poor writers have written if they had received such a huge sum of money? Novakovich has written too little to justify such good fortune. He has lived too comfortably and sold himself to the Americans, and therefore is incapable of seeing things clearly without bias in the tough and unforgiving Balkans." So, in a story in which I describe a Serbian siege of Vukovar, I was criticized for trying to find some redeeming traits in a Serbian soldier. I alienated the nationalists by not writing exclusively from the Croatian point of view, and some of the leftists simply by being an American, which, when I am in Croatia, I feel I am. Of course, in America I feel Croatian. I am hyphenated, between the two cultures, and I will never integrate the two, but will suffer always from multicultural schizophrenia, or rather, bicultural psychosis.

From strangers I got many compliments on my work, but my old friends, except for one, a concert pianist, either abstained from commenting, except very minimally—for example: "It's readable." Several of them complained that I had written about the war so much. "Why, the war does not matter to you?" I asked.

"Oh yes, it does, but I'm sick of it. It's too ugly."

"Should I write only about pretty subjects?"

"But why write about wars? Is that all Americans are interested in? Croatian violence?"

"I write what I write because of what I want to understand, not for a market. I don't have a market or an audience."

That I claim to not write for a definable market baffles them, since clearly I don't write a literature of beautiful effects and I don't experiment enough to claim a niche in the avant-garde I disappoint my friends by not being a rich and slick writer or a flamboyant stylist. People here read a lot of Robert Ludlum, John Grisham, and other bestselling Americans, and a small coterie measures all new writing by the standard of Nabokov and Carver.

During the communist years, the country was in love with America, but now there is a surprising amount of anti-American sentiment from the right and the left. The nationalists resent America because of The Hague prosecutions and the perception that America has meddled in the elections here. The leftists mimic the general European disgust with Bush and American military supremacy and environmental insensitivity. Only pro-business centrists seem to like the States, but even among them there is a sense of disenchantment with America, which promised so much in terms of free market investment and which does so little now. Unlike in Slovenia, there's hardly any investment from the States here although the new government is mostly centrist and slightly leftist. It's certainly a reformed government, with the nationalists in the subordinate role, and at the moment it seems to be one of the most liberal regimes in the former communist block.

The shift to the left was a revolt against the regressive and nationalist leader Franjo Tudjman, who had usurped all the power and stolen a fair share of the treasury. A perception reigned before the election that with a liberal government, foreign aid would pour into Croatia. The timing may be to blame. Europe is in recession right now, and Serbia's pro-democracy track is a better attention getter. There are few new ventures in Europe now, and the States are in a downturn too. But it may be also that Croatia's image has been Nazified so much that it is hard to convince the world that there is anything progressive here. The old regime made sure not to emphasize the leftist history of Croatia: the inception of the communist movement in Yugoslavia here, Tito's (he was a Croat) strong partisan and anti-Ustasha and anti-Nazi activity, and even Tudjman's being an anti-Nazi general whose family members had been killed by the Ustashas in World War Two. Before his death in December 1999, the fiftieth anniversary of the victory over Nazism, Tudjman was shunned by all the European leaders, although he was the only head of state who had been an active participant in the struggle against Hitler! Because of his stubbornness in pursuing the national liberation of Croatia from communist Yugoslavia, he deliberately understated his communist credentials and isolated Croatia from the West, and now the isolationism sticks.

Going back to the issue of global anti-Americanism: a friend of mine—a bookstore owner and publisher—tells me that he has a very bad impression of American journalists. Sasha had been drafted into the Croatian army in 1991 and again in 1995. A correspondent for the *New York Times* was going to conduct interviews at the Hotel Intercontinental, and Sasha looked forward to being able to talk in depth about the war for such an important newspaper.

They sat down, ordered coffee, and the American journalist opened the interview, "So, how many Serbs have you killed?"

Sasha replied, "You can fuck yourself," and left. He complained to me, "What does the guy think, that he is a judge from The Hague and we are all war criminals? When you see that he has a bias and agenda, what's the point of talking? And even with an agenda, he could show more respect. These guys have an attitude that we are savages and they are Lords or something."

I asked him, "Well, how was the campaign?"

"For my unit, it was a ghost campaign. We traveled from one empty village to another. The Serbian population and the army had withdrawn prior to our coming. And it was better that way. Now they can come back—at least they are alive. Who knows how it would have been if we had to fight door to door? Anyway, their total withdrawal before our arrival was a brilliant chess move. Now they can claim we ethnically cleansed the region. It will be impossible to prove that it was not ethnic cleansing. So, they will have all the legal rights to return, with more than equal rights for employment and welfare checks. In other words, what they had under communism when they had nearly all the best jobs they will have again.

Brilliant."

I asked him a rude question as well, but it was strategically placed as merely a stone in the flux of conversation. "Do you hate Serbs?"

"I used to, especially in 1991, when they destroyed everything and we had to crouch in trenches and hide. I had to train myself not to hate them."

He nevertheless followed their literature, and enthusiastically recommended the new Serbian writer Vladiar Arsenijevic to me. When Belgrade had a book expo a couple of years ago, he went there, representing Croatian publishers. Even the Serb extreme right-wing Chetnik leader, Vojislav Seselj, came to his stall and said, "Nice exhibit, lots of pretty Serbian books."

Sasha had the opportunity to get back at me when race riots broke out in Cincinnati. We spent the evening discussing American racism, and the whole time Sasha had a self-satisfied look of vindication, as though savoring the Biblical maxim, "He among you who is blameless, let him cast the first stone."

I explained that most of the professors at the university lived in the white suburbs and then criticized the working-class whites who lived in mixed neighborhoods and the police, who worked in the ghetto, for being racist. Kind of like Icelanders criticizing people in the Balkans for not getting along. "Do you think Richard Holbrooke lives in a ghetto?" Sasha asked.

One person who seems to be universally hated is Slobadan Milosevic. After Milosevic was handed over to The Hague, a cousin of mine, a car mechanic, told me that the maximum sentence of fifty years that The Hague could impose would do just fine, essentially a life-sentence. (As I write, the War Crimes Tribunal sentenced the Serbian general in charge of the Srebenica massacre of Muslims with genocide, and gave him forty-six years in jail. I wonder why not fifty?) Other people wished he could be shot like Nicholae Ceaucescu was in Romania. But a few friends said, "Well, why don't they bring in the United States Senator John Kerry and former Russian President Boris Yeltsin? Those two are war criminals, too, but it will never happen because they come from power-ful nations."

The world, which was so lackadaisical when high U.S., British, and French officials did whatever they could to make sure Milosevic would not be disturbed in his aggression, now seems to be eager to act in the safe court, but first they should try those in power who made the aggression possible—James Baker, George H.W. Bush, and John Major. James Baker gave Belgrade the green light for the aggression in 1991 when Slovenia and Croatia declared independence by stating in Belgrade that Yugoslavia had the right to do whatever it took to preserve its unity. Still, people in Croatia loved seeing pictures of a fatter and grayer Milosevic in prison.

Now that two Croatian generals have been indicted and "invited" to The Hague, the prevailing sentiment is against the Tribunal. People of most political parties agree that The Hague, by trying the general who was in charge of the war in Krajina in 1995—when Croatia in three days, with tacit and not so tacit American support defeated the self-proclaimed Serb Republic of Krajina—has criminalized the war of liberation which Croatia led to restore sovereignty over the territory within its internationally recognized borders. Before that, Croatia was cut in half, and the Croatian population had been ethnically cleansed, thousands killed, and driven out of the region. In 1995, after the massacre of Srebenica, in which 8,000 Muslim men were killed by Serbian soldiers within the UN Safe Haven, there was a threat of a bigger massacre if the town of Bihac in Bosnia, along the Croatian border, fell. NATO generals estimated at the time that half a million soldiers were needed to prevent the catastrophe, and it could not get them anywhere, so it invited Croatia to intervene, to break the siege by penetrating through Krajina, and Croatia did that, thus saving that part of Bosnia. Unfortunately a mass exodus of the Serbian population ensued, some 120,000 people fleeing the region, and that is one aspect of the war that needs to be redressed.

To be accepted into the "civilized" world (which part of the world is not civilized?), Croatia will have to demonstrate a non-chauvinist politics, with the expelled Serbs actively beseeched to return. Many are returning, but slowly. My sister-in-law, who is from Serbia, says that her relatives travel to the former Krajina (everything is former here) without any troubles and have been doing that since 1996. I come from one part of what was once Krajina, the former Austrian Military Border, which was composed of a mixed population: Serbs, Croats, Czechs, and Hungarians. The region was never predominantly Serbian, so to turn it into an independent country along ethnic lines in order to annex it to Greater Serbia made no sense, just as it made no sense to annex Silesia to Germany around the issue of there being multitudes of Germans in Silesia. Germany lost that argument, and two million Germans were expelled from the Czech Republic without any redress. After that huge ethnic cleansing campaign Czechs now build walls to keep gypsies at one end of a village, to segregate them. Yet it seems the Czechs enjoy a reputation for being among the gentlest and the most progressive peoples of the world. "Why is that?" I asked Ivan Klima at the Toronto International Festival of Authors when we talked about chauvinism in the Balkans. "How come Czechs are so chauvinistic?" He disagreed with me and gave me some fuzzy legal explanation why the conflict with gypsies occurred. I was astonished: he seemed to legitimize it.

The return of expelled populations is going too slowly in Bosnia, as well as in Croatia and Serbia. So when I went to my hometown, I drove through Novska and north, where Serbs had the eastern part of their Republic of Krajina. They had destroyed many Croatian villages. Then Croats took over the region and destroyed many Serbian villages. So for about fifteen miles I drove through a ghost country. Of more than two hundred houses, perhaps five were whole and inhabited. The natural setting is amazingly beautiful, with lush fields and oak forests on a mountainous terrain, yet because of incomplete de-mining, you can't simply hike and bird-watch and go mushroom gathering there, although that is precisely what I always do when I visit the spot with my friend, Boris.

So far so good. Now that I have declared my political positions perhaps I have undermined my letter and become an unreliable narrator. I wish I had spent more time writing about mushrooms than about politics, but what can I do? Just in case you are interested in mushrooms, I will say that Boris and I found on several occasions more oyster mushrooms on old beeches than we could pick. Another time, we found several pounds of *lactarius deliciosus*. And on another visit, we found lots of chantarelles and King Boletes. We fried most of them in olive oil with onions and had our primitive fun, eating from our earth, sometimes with bits of the earth. Boris claims that he knows where the mines are, that they are only in the marginal territory between the Border Region (Krajina) and the rest, like double borders. Deep in the forest you are all right, he claims. Here the biggest danger are the boars, who dig through the ground undisturbed by hunters who had nearly exterminated them before the recent wars.

I went to the Pakrac hospital to visit my mother, who was recovering from her heart attack. In *1991*, Serbian soldiers nearly destroyed the hospital, and now, ten years later, the hospital is still not restored, except for one small building out of half a dozen. It seems a strange place to seek recovery, with its window view of buildings with howitzer holes in them, but it's the closest hospital to Daruvar, and my brother, who used to be a doctor there, still has friends working in it. Nevertheless, driving by the ghastly and overgrown hospital wings did not put me in an optimistic frame of mind. No wonder that even she could not forget politics and while watching TV asked me, being worldly, to explain to her why the world did not think it was right that Croatia defend itself. Did everybody except Croatia have a right to self-defense and self-determination? She wept while she asked these questions, and taking a look through the windows at the destroyed hospital, I did not know how to reply except to say that she had overdosed on the Croatia-as-victim perspective from TV, that the world actually did not care whether Croatia defended itself or not, that most of the people in the States did not know where Croatia was and in fact, many commentators confused it with Serbia and others thought it was part of the former Soviet Union. Consoling as it might be to imagine that people in America followed the fortunes of Croatia very closely, in fact hardly anybody cared. Well, Croatia could defend itself. But that does not mean that Croatia should not eagerly bring to court all those who committed war crimes. Many soldiers fought out of love for liberty, but many did commit atrocities—some out of personal revenge since their family members had been slaughtered by Serbs, and some did it who knows why—and all of them should be punished. Not that wars can be fought in a fair fashion according to a chivalric code, but even that illusion is better than condoning soldiers' cruelty and madness.

The recovery in general seems to be progressing here way too slowly. The Croats expelled from the rural Posavina region in the Republika Srpska in Bosnia do not go back, nor do the Croats expelled from Central Bosnia. Serbs have not come back to the villages in Western Slavonia in Croatia; they come back only to towns, in small numbers. Mines are still waiting for the returning exiles in many of their favored landscapes.

On the other hand, significant portions of Croatia never had much war, and if the country is not thriving, it's not doing worse than it did in years gone by. I am writing from the Croatian island of Hvar, a beautiful resort with many yachts in the harbor. Steven Spielberg was in Dubrovnik on the mainland. Tourism is thriving along the coast. The war interrupted it for a while but the country looks all the better for lying fallow, with fewer factories emitting pollution. Croatia is a land of many worlds; this one is Mediterranean. My home town is basically Hungarian and Central European. We are here because my son is taking lessons in a music camp. His favorite teacher, Vladimir Perlin from Byelorussia, is instructing him in the cello. He is a charismatic teacher, who plays with finesse and powerful expressiveness, and only because he is allergic to rosin is he not a renowned soloist. And I have a task, to write an article for the *New York Times* travel section about the island. That will be much harder than writing this letter, since I will have to keep politics out and present the sunny side.

Well, here at the coast, there is a lot of sunny side, unlike inland. Last night we visited a ghost village here, with many houses falling apart. (Wait, that does not sound sunny, but it will be!) Only one couple lives in a house on the hill overlooking the ocean. We climbed through narrow cobbled streets, admiring old stone buildings with even the roof-tiles made out of stone glaring in the sun, and saw an open kitchen with a fireplace and old utensils, but no souls. Two dogs came out to growl at us, but then began to give us presents, bones from their digs. We petted them. We heard you could ask a day in advance to have a meal in a makeshift restaurant, and the man will go out in a boat, catch fish, and grill it for you, and give you his homemade red wine, for very little money. So, that's our plan for tonight, to have a fresh meal in a ghost village overlooking the Adriatic in the full moonlight. Odysseus, according to a few scholars, got lost in the Adriatic. The sieges are over, so one can think of beauty and poetry for an evening.

Now weeks have passed. That beauty soon disappeared. The following day we got news that most subsidies for medicine would be slashed, so poor people will no longer be able to afford life-saving medicine. One woman said, "I'll have to quit buying bread, so I can buy lipostatins." And suddenly, the phone rates tripled, so they are now much more expensive than in Western Europe. Croatia sold its phone communications system to Deutsche Telekom, which, facing bankruptcy, wants to milk from this poor country as much money as possible without competition and regulation. Sure, Croatia needs foreign investment, and the government liberalized the laws, but there is a difference between investment and exploitative takeover. Now the country is up for grabs by foreign corporate vultures. In that sense, the new regime, while pretending to be leftist, accomplishes what a right-wing, laissez-faire system would: no protection for the workers and the population in general. I think the people would mount a socialist revolution at this point if they had any will left over from the wars. From my perspective, Croatian independence is an illusion; it will be a colony again, this time of the large corporations and wealthy investors who are busy buying up all the islands.

Well, Larry, I don't know whether this is the kind of letter you were looking for. Let me know, and I hope to see you in a few months. We'll find a Mediterranean-style restaurant in Ann Arbor, or wherever we meet, and it will be my turn to cover the bill.

Note: This letter was written to Lawrence Goldstein, editor of the *Michigan Quarterly Review.*

A TRAIN ROMANCE

My family—wife Jeanette and two kids, Joseph, seven, and Eva, three—were to take a train from Zagreb to Daruvar early in the morning. Actually, not that early: 7:55. I woke up at five, and at six I shook Jeanette out of her sleep. She said, "Do I really have to wake up?"

"We have to go to Daruvar."

"Can't we skip it?"

"No, the kids want to see Grandma, and they want to play with Boris and his son. The last time it was all too brief. You are the one who suggested it!"

I boiled water and made Turkish-style coffee out of French roast beans we had brought from the States, and Jeanette sat up to drink it, but soon, laid it aside to sleep again. I persevered in waking her up, and then I woke up Joey. Eva we could carry, so she kept sleeping. Joey squealed out of unhappiness. Still, the idea of playing with little Franjo on a farm on a hillside with lots of sheep, ducks, in vineyards and orchards gave him some fortitude, so pretty soon he grinned and bore the discomfort of walking through the dusty street, toward the tram stop. The street was made of asphalt, cement, and brick, without a trace of vegetation, as some kind of concrete corridor for trams, cars, and pedestrians. At the corner of

Selska, near a *pekarna* (bakery), we waited. The smells of fresh bread and pastries invited me to inhale deeply for the first time that warm morning. That was one good thing about Zagreb: almost every block had a bakery with fresh loaves and *piroshka*s. Soon, a blue tram, number nine, wobbled and squealed to a stop and we climbed on it. It clanked in its slow way, and Joey sat on the sunny side. Jeanette said, "You could sit in the shady row." Joey stood up, walked across the aisle, and as he was about to sit down the tram screeched to a stop. Joey fell, and hit the railing with his forehead, above his right eye, over the brow. He screamed. We lifted him. The spot was pale and red, with a scrape, and it seemed it was swelling swiftly. He nearly vomited.

"Are you all right?" Jeanette asked. "Oh my God, he's hurt!"

"Yes, but he hasn't lost his consciousness," I said.

"Shut up. He's hurt. We can't go to Daruvar now."

"Are you sure? Kids recover fast."

Joey cried and his brow looked swollen.

"No, we have to go back home," she said.

"OK, let's get off the tram and go to the other side of the street to catch another tram back."

"No, he can't move now. We can just sit."

"Till when?"

"Till the tram makes the full circle and then we'll get off."

"That would take more than an hour, and if he's hurt, he could use the time better."

We managed to get off at the train station. Joey didn't look that bad to me. "Let's give it a shot," I said. "He'll feel better in Daruvar."

"You want to torture him like this? How beastly of you."

"That's childhood. What kind of childhood would it be without black eyes? By his age, I'd had a dozen."

"I don't doubt that—and some lasting brain damage, obviously."

Joey stood up and whimpered, without much conviction in his own pain.

"Look, he's standing fine. He's not dizzy. He'll make it. We get him some ice, slap it on his forehead, and off we go."

Concerned Mom prevailed, and soon we were back on the tram in the other direction. By the time we reached home, Joey was teasing his little sister and laughing.

We unlocked the door and turned off the alarm. My aunt, who lived on the first floor, was absolutely terrified of burglars; the house was broken into twice before the alarm was installed. We climbed the stairs made out of slippery pink marble from the island of Brac, the kind that Tito had used in his villas. My brother had bought the marble at a discount from a patient of his and built the staircase and added two floors to the house, and we rented the second floor from him. We walked back to the darkened apartment, in an already hot morning, and as we sprawled over the beds, we agreed, "This feels better than sitting on a smoky train."

Actually, I was pleased. Now I didn't know why I had pushed the trip. True, our trip to Daruvar two weeks before was fun, but the weather was tolerable then. For a while, the first trip had been pleasant indeed. We had a compartment to ourselves, opened the window wide, and watched fields of red poppies in radiant green fields. We pulled all the velvet seats together, and the kids had a little gym, leaping and rolling, until a jaunty man, about my age but certainly in much better shape, walked into our compartment. He talked in Croatian—which meant I was the only one who could converse with him—asking us where we were going, and told us he was an engine man. He had driven the same train to Zagreb, and now his colleague would drive it back while he relaxed.

"Joey, this man is the engine man, the first one you've ever met," I said. Joey had watched Thomas the Tank Engine series passionately when he was two and three years old, and he had to have replicas of all the engines and coaches. For a whole year, he thought he was a train engine, Gordon #4. Now, however, Joey didn't show any enthusiasm, sore that he couldn't keep leaping all over the compartment. The engineer talked about his sons, how they loved to travel with him, and how he let them hoot, press the brakes, and so on. He said everything about the job was great, except the pay, about two hundred dollars a month, and he added, "That's pretty good. My neighbors make much less. And may I ask, how much do you make in the States?"

When I answered, he frowned. Soon he left our compartment without saying good-bye. Envy, or hatred of America, or sorrow for his own country's poverty, or all of the above, got him. I was annoyed. I should not have told him anything. After all, my academic salary was just that: academic. I saw him sulking by himself in another compartment.

At one point, we smelled smoke. The train jerked forward a few times in loud bangs, and then stopped again, with the smoke engulfing us. I walked into the corridor and saw the engine man step outside the coach to talk with his colleague. Thick steamy smoke hissed out of the engine.

"The engine caught on fire," said our engine man. "But don't worry, *narode*, everything is under control. The flames are out!"

The passengers didn't seem to worry anyway. They didn't swear, as I had expected them to. They must have been used to such little incidents. Joey said, "Will it explode?" with a note of delight in his voice. I wondered: Had our fatherly traveling companion set the engine on fire, out of sheer hate of American prosperity? I doubted it. He couldn't have gone to the front of the train so fast. Who knows how old the engine was, plus, on such low salaries, the engineers probably hadn't bothered to change the oil and to clean the engine.

By the time the replacement engine came, we missed our connecting train, but Boris picked us up and took us to his farm. He is a gentleman peasant. He teaches literature in Osijek, and most of the week tills the fields and takes care of his five cows. Anyway, this time we would not be going to Daruvar. No poppy fields and fires for us.

I called up Boris and my brother to announce we wouldn't be coming. Boris said, "Well, I could drive to pick you up, in the early afternoon." I checked with the family, and to them it sounded all right.

What would we do the whole sweltering Saturday otherwise? The heat soon got into the apartment. Just boiling water on the stove produced much of it, and the walls had been gathering heat for days, and without the open windows, the heat got trapped in the apartment. With the open windows, even greater heat would get into the apartment. So perhaps the ride would not be too bad, even though Boris kept the windows on his car closed because he believed, like most people in Croatia, that drafts were dangerous, even in the heat. People rode buses with all the windows closed, without air conditioning. They did not believe in deodorant. For that matter, I didn't either, but I did have second and third thoughts when stuck in a sweaty crowd. And the idea that Boris should drive for four hours to get us to Daruvar—too much sacrifice on his part. Once we got excited again about Daruvar, I called up the train station information. There were two trains going pretty close to Daruvar, where Boris could easily pick us up.

"Why do we always get to the train station too early?" asked Jeanette. "Isn't it enough to go half an hour before the train departs?"

"Yes, early in the morning it is, when there are no crowds in the streets."

"But it's Saturday; there can't be any rush hour."

And so we went half an hour before the train at 11:30 would depart.

While buying apple strudels, cherry turnovers, and walnut and poppy pastry, we missed one number nine and waited for another, and it came soon enough, five minutes later. We would probably make it. At one stop, the tram made three or four stops: one before it, because there was one tram ahead, then at the stop, the doors opened again, and we waited for a couple of minutes, then it sopped again when someone waved from the sidewalk after the designated stop, and then the lights changed to red. After that, on the green light, just as the tram lurched forward, an old car stalled on the tracks, and by the time it moved, we were waiting for the new red light to turn. We got to the train station several minutes after

11:30, and Jeanette insisted that we run. The sun was already blazing, and just a minute of running got us nearly drenched. I stopped to read the train schedule. "No time for that," shouted Jeanette.

"What do you mean no time? We have to know from what platform the train departs."

"It's a small country; there aren't that many options."

"There are," I said. I noticed that the train was listed as departing from the third platform. We ran through the underpass. The train was not in sight. It had clearly departed. Jeanette didn't believe it. "How could they depart on time? I thought everything here was late."

"They could, when you don't want them to," I said. "Sometimes they leave early, just for the hell of it."

"How about this train, where is it going?"

"To Osijek, the northern route, nowhere near Novska. We are better off waiting for another train. But here, this one goes to Budapest, that wouldn't be too bad, would it?"

"I am hungry. I think we are all hungry."

Now one restaurant served only drinks. Another one had two dining rooms: one was a big cloud of cigarette smoke and the other one, with the bathroom on one end and the kitchen on the other, blended the smells of both, with urine and smoke from grilled pork dominating. With our stomachs turning, we went outdoors and had Cokes, while a couple at a table next to ours talked on cell phones, each to someone else. Seemed like a good relationship to me; at least they wouldn't quarrel with each other. They could coexist, parallel talk on microwaves, cooking their brains.

The waitress wouldn't come out into the street to collect the money. That was one frustrating thing about cafés in Zagreb: you might be lucky enough to place your order in five minutes, but the waiters hardly ever of their initiative came to give you the bill, and if they did, they didn't bother to come to collect the money, and you had to track them down somewhere to push money onto them. Forget about quick drinks. Espresso, after all does mean in English adaptation "express, fast" coffee, but there is no such thing as getting it fast. In one café next door to our apartment, when I got my espresso, I finished it in one gulp and wanted to pay immediately, but the waitress said, "Where I come from in Bosnia, we consider that rude to finish coffee fast. You got to savor it, caress it, chat. You can't just leave."

"That is all very nice," I said, "but I have to rush now." As I walked out of that café, I thought," What would we chat about?" I would probably want to ask her about how she suffered in Bosnia, whether anybody in her family was murdered or had murdered, how and when she got to Croatia, and so on, but that would be rude, and it wouldn't be light enough to count as a chat. Anyway, now we did manage to wave the waitress over. She petted Joey on the head. He is blond, and wherever we go people pet him on the head, and he shrieks.

We still had plenty of time to catch the third train. I carried Eva on my neck, and Jospeh cried that he was hot and tired. We ate at the huge dining hall in the train station. We were the only customers. Joseph liked to eat shish kebabs, and so we ordered some. They were quite red, from paprika. Jeanette wouldn't allow Joseph to eat that since she had read that Hungarian paprika often contained lead, for bright red coloring. I remembered the days when the dining room was full. Since the break-up of Yugoslavia, the international trains to Greece and Turkey quit passing through. They now went through Hungary and Romania. In addition to that, the bad reputation of Croatia with its nationalistic regime scared people off. Even though Croatia had now the most leftist government in the former Yugoslavia and nothing resembling a war, and even though the place was amazingly safe—kids walked to school unaccompanied by adults, and you could see them anywhere, even late in the evening—the image of Croatia was apparently highly unappealing despite the more than one thousand islands in the Adriatic. I had never seen Zagreb so provincial. Hardly anywhere would you see tourists, or overhear people speaking in English. At the train station, in the heat, prevailed a defeated atmosphere of boredom. Peasants waited patiently and gingerly chewed bread.

Policemen strolled on the front platform, smoking short cigarettes. During the Yugoslav regime, they could randomly ID anybody in the crowd, and that gave them something to do. Now, they had to be polite, which left them at a loss. A diesel engine shunted coaches nearby, emitting smoke and rumbling the platform.

I bought tickets to Banova Jaruga.

The train was at the farthest platform: extension A. After a good walk, we got to the train on time. The third time. It felt idiotic, and it was, to need three tries to finally make it to the train on time. The train was nearly full. It was a passenger train, without compartments. Each coach was one big room, with closed windows. They could not be opened much, only a square foot on the top. Basically, the coaches resembled buses strung together. People inside gasped for air, sweat poured down their faces, their shirts were wet around the armpits. Nearly all the seats were taken. Jeanette and I looked inside with despair, exchanged a look, and she said, "No way. You expect me to boil there for an hour and a half? No way."

Some people waved newspapers to move the air. Most passengers had their mouths open, and for a moment, the train looked to me like an aquarium full of fish opening and closing their mouths, for illusory air. The people looked like fish out of the water, flapping their gills in the steam. And to bring little children into that sweat, a room of about 120 degrees Farenheit, into a segment of portable Dachau? That would be criminal.

"I agree," I said. "No way."

So we walked back. We felt a little liberated, despite the embarrassing futility. What a way to spend a life—walk back and forth, between trams and train stations, without getting anywhere.

On the way through the waiting room, it occurred to me that we probably never would use the ticket, so I asked for reimbursement. The counter at which I had bought the tickets was closed, although the young lady was still there, staring off into space.

I asked at the counter next to it to get reimbursed for the ticket.

"Where did you get it?" a clerk with bronze-colored hair asked.

"Right here."

"No, you didn't."

"All right, at this counter, right next to yours. It's all one and the same thing, isn't it?"

"When?"

"Can't you see? It's printed on the ticket. Just ten minutes ago. Can I have the money back? It's too hot to travel today."

"Not at this counter. You could come back when that one is open."

"But she is still here, the same salesperson," I said, and pointed to the woman who kept sitting and staring like a wax figure. I did a double take to assess whether she was alive. Come back? To waste another hour. And who is to say that it's going to be open then?

"You can go to the information desk and fill out the reimbursement form, stating clearly why you are returning the tickets, and then you will get reimbursed, all but ten percent."

Now, with my family totally out of sorts, to wait in lines, fill out forms, show IDs, talk to grumpy clerks, no thanks. So I tore the ticket, and flung it over the glass window to the clerk, and said something unprintable. She looked surprised, as I was. I did not expect myself capable of such native vocabulary. But at the moment, sacrificing six dollars seemed well worth the freedom of expression. Cathartic anger. We went out of the train station, onto a tram, with the romance of public transportation waning. No wonder that, even though the country grew poorer, there were fewer and fewer trains scheduled and more and more cars everywhere. Now I suggested that we all go to Sljeme, the mountain outside Zagreb, in a cable car, but the family said, "Enough travel."

"What travel?" I said. "We haven't traveled anywhere."

"You figured that one out," Jeanette joked. It seemed the family won. I could not take them anywhere, the beauty of trains notwithstanding. What happened to the damned trains? I used to love to hop on them and drift through the land. I no longer drank, and now I could not ride trains...what pleasures were left?

ON FINDING
A GRAVE IN CLEVELAND

One version of the promised land, of course, is America, and my father often dreamed of going to it. My grandmother had died in Cleveland, and nobody in my family—most of them living in Croatia and none in the States—knew where her grave was. I couldn't find the records in the downtown library in Cleveland.

I visited the old house on Carry Avenue where she used to live. Before World War II, the block had burned down on one end of the street because the gas tanks there exploded and many Slovenes and Croats who lived on the street were killed. Now, at one end of the street, there was a new park, Grdina Park, after a Slovenian priest by the same name who had buried many of the victims. Grd means ugly, so the park has been appropriately named.

Even twenty-five years ago when I visited the States for the first time, the neighborhood, as the first sight of the glorious country for me, a Balkan provincial, appalled me. Rusty factories with shattered windows, orange-brown rails overgrown in weeds, houses with caving porches. The old Croats and Slovenes spoke a strange language, a mixture of English and Croatian, and both languages were ungrammatical, or in a way, they had their own grammar: Cronglish, or Slonglish, one could name the language if there were enough people speaking it. And there, in that neighborhood, my grandfather had worked and wasted his health, acquiring chronic bronchitis in a screw factory, along with many of his compatriots. According to letters Cleveland immigrant workers sent to Croatia at the beginning of the century, the smoke arising from more than a thousand chimneys was so heavy that one could rarely see the sky.

My grandfather never liked Cleveland. Once Yugoslavia was formed in 1918, he decided to go back and enjoy the pan-Slavic state. He planned to become a big-time farmer, American style, but he over-estimated what his savings could do. He went to a village, Medjuric, and wouldn't budge from it, even though he was a poor peasant, having chosen sandy soil that alternately flooded and dried up, and yielded more frogs than cornstalks. He wheezed in the fields, happy that he did not have to go to a stultifying factory in Cleveland. He read, talked, and joked, and I remember him as a tall, jovial and emaciated man. He died when I was seven.

His was the first in the line of many funerals in my childhood. He was buried next to the train tracks, so every time I took the train, I'd lean out the window and see Pavlo Bubanovic on black marble. This gave me some satisfaction. So, I thought, these are my roots, next to the rails, inviting me to uproot myself.

Anyway, Mary Volcensek, my grandmother, had left him before his death, right after World War II. She loved the war years so much that in Cleveland, while working as a cashier at the May Company, she read all the Second World War novels she could find. She easily talked about the war, the wormy gangrenes she as a nurse had attended to on partisans' legs, the warm handshake Tito had given her. In the States, she never accumulated any property because she gave away everything she had to her sons in Croatia, and much less to my mother.

She lived first with a priest who had an altar in the house and held private services in Latin, and she laughed at his religion good-humoredly. She spent a lot of time walking from one friend to another. I visited her after she had her first heart attack at the age of seventy-six. She said she had no desire to live, and she refused to eat, trying to die, but after the second heart attack, doctors revived her again. The third did it.

At the time I lived without money and jobs in New York City, so I did not go to the funeral. She was buried by her older brother, who'd had a stroke, and his wife, Stephanie. She was incensed that she'd had two sick old people on her hands to deal with, and now a burial to boot. She shouted at me on the phone, so I didn't call her to ask her where my grandmother was buried, and when I tried later on, her number was not listed.

Now, fifteen years later, in 1999, I was sure I would find Stephanie in the same house, or somewhere else in the city, and she would tell me how to find my grandmother's grave, after rightly rebuking me for neglecting the funeral. Plus, she would probably want me to pay for part of the expenses, which would be all right. I had just received a Guggenheim fellowship, and although I hadn't written in the application that I would pay for debts on my grand-mother's funeral, I was sure the Foundation couldn't object to such a use of part of the money.

I came to the one-story white house with wooden siding, and in the yard was a man I didn't know washing a car. He didn't know anything about the Volcenseks.

"Who are you looking for?" asked a woman from across the street.

"Mary Volcensek used to live here. I am her nephew. I would like to..."

"Oh, she died."

"I know. I am looking for her relatives."

"They died. Everybody in that house died. They all died within a year."

"Stephanie too?"

"Yea, she died of cancer."

"Do you know any of her relatives?"

"Well, yeah, I am her niece."

"Do you know where Mary is buried."

"I have no idea."

"Who would know?"

"Maybe my other aunt. She's a bartender at..." She gave me a name of a bar on St. Clair and 72nd.

I drove there. It was a strange dive, with deer heads, pool table, and many old men. The aunt had a husky voice, broken down by too much smoking.

"I have no idea where she's buried. But you could talk with my cousin, Babe. Babe knows everybody in the neighborhood."

"Where does she live? What's her address?"

"Her last name is Cizel. You can look it up in the book."

I did, and I drove to the house, but there was nobody there. Another white house, near 55th, on Bona, near the Sterle Slovenian Restaurant, where many weddings were held, and where I was defeated in my attempts to become a vegetarian. I had been one for a month, but now, during the break in my search for my grandmother's grave, I couldn't resist veal goulash. The best veal goulash I've ever had. Later I couldn't repeat the experience at the same place. I am sure that the breakdown of my resolve had much to do with the pleasure of that initial meal—I savored the juices with onions and soft Italian bread.... Anyway, after that I tried to find the old woman, Babe, but she wasn't there.

I went to the Slovenian Catholic Church, St. Vitius, two blocks away, although I thought that was hopeless since my mother was a Baptist who did not attend churches, although she later attended a Lutheran church for the lunch program for the elderly. My wife and my kids accompanied me, and the kids chased each other in the parish office, while I tried to calm them down. A young woman showed up and gave me the parish records to look through. And sure enough, I found Mary Volcensek's name in the book. The priest walked in, a serious and sad Slovene in his later forties, and he said, "Oh yes, Mary and her brother John. They died within a couple of weeks. That's an incredibly sad story."

When I asked him to tell me more, he wouldn't.

But he gave me the directions to the Calvary Cemetery and said that the office there would be able to direct me to the location of her grave; they would have the records of her section and lot numbers.

I tried calling the office but got no response.

On the way there, we stopped by the Cizel's again. Upon my ringing at the door, an old woman's face appeared and I recognized it. My grandmother and I had spent an evening with her twenty-five years earlier, during Nixon's resignation address. But that was in a different house.

"Oh, you are from the old country, aren't you?" She asked. "Come in!"

I introduced myself, and she said, "I remember you."

I was delighted for a moment to be in the world in which memory does not fail; or rather, after many failures, the memory resurfaces and brings us together again. My enthusiasm in memory was dimmed a little when she asked me how my father in Zagreb was. I realized she took me for my cousin, who had visited with along his father. "Oh, you mean my Uncle Ivo. He's dead. Bled to death from an ulcer. And his son Damir, he's doing well. Married, has a daughter..."

"Oh, that's it, Damir."

"Yes, you mistook me for Damir," I said. "But I visited you too, three years before he did."

"Oh, yes, now I remember. I remember that evening..."

And I think she did. Her mind seemed to be quite together.

"And this is your family. Lovely children," she said. My six-year-old son hid behind my wife. Eva, my two-year-old, ran in circles around the room.

There was an old woman with Babe, her mother. Babe was seventy and her mother ninety-seven. As renters, they lived together on the ground floor, which they kept perfectly clean.

Babe brought out a box with papers, death records, and photographs.

"She goes to all the funerals around here," her mother said.

"Somebody has to," she said. "Many of our old friends have died, and some without anybody to take care of the funeral arrangements, so I help the priest out that way."

"Oh, and she goes to the gravestones, and pulls out the weeds, cleans the stones."

"Yes, but we haven't been to your grandmother's grave in half a year. We'd like to go, but we just got back from a dentist's appointment. Can you believe it, my mom has such good teeth that she still gets toothaches. You wouldn't think that was a good sign but it is: her teeth are alive. So we had to go to a dentist to fill a cavity. Oh my, that was a journey. See, we don't have a car, so we walk everywhere and we take buses. But next time you come to Cleveland, let us know, and we'll all go."

"Are you hungry? Would you like to eat some Slovenian sausages?"

"Yes. We saw the Slovenian grocery on the corner on the way here," I said.

"Their sausages are the best," she said.

"How about some beer?" She brought out some Heineken beer.

I was impressed. The ladies were aging with style.

"Oh, no wonder you have lived to be over ninety-seven," I said to Babe's mother.

"I never drink," she said. "The priest visited us, and for some reason he brought us this, so whenever a guest comes, we hope to make him drink some. We had a dozen, now eight to go yet."

They boiled the sausages for Jeanette and me. We enjoyed eating them with sauerkraut. "Won't you join us?" I said.

"Oh no," said the older one. "We have sausages just for guests. I haven't eaten one in years."

"She just eats bread, crackers, fruits, and salads," said Babe.

The old woman was smiling happily at us. I was a bit disenchanted with their healthy example; I prefer to see people stay healthy and eat and drink and be merry, but here they were merry enough without heavy food and drink. In fact, they were merrier than most people I had talked with in days.

The old woman remembered my grandmother, for they would be now the same age, and even better, she remembered her family and her mother. "They were our neighbors just a couple of blocks from here. You could see Katarina walk barefoot even in the winter. She was a strong woman. She gave birth to her children while men were at work, and then she'd cook a meal for them, so once they came back from the factory, they'd have something to eat. And then, she'd go back to her baby. I don't think she ever saw a doctor."

"She wore shoes only when she went to St. Clair Avenue—for her that was the high society, and she didn't want to look like a peasant there. She liked walking barefoot because she saved on shoes that way."

Wow, that was great. She was remembering my great-grandmother, and she would have probably come up with more details if Babe hadn't insisted on dominating the conversation and on talking about St. Vitius church, which I didn't mind, just having seen what great service the church provided: it buried even those who didn't pay any dues, and it kept records.

Now and then, Babe would interrupt her mother: "Oh, Mama, you don't remember it right." Then she'd turn to us, and say, "You know just lately her mind has been going."

The old woman would smile knowingly. It didn't seem to me that her mind was going. She looked alert and clever.

"And she doesn't watch out enough for herself. A couple of summers ago, we still didn't have air-conditioning—thank god, now we do—and one hot night, I found her asleep on the floor with the front door open right into the street. Someone could have come in…"

"Oh, at my age, how could I fear that?" asked the old woman.

"How did you like school? What subject did you like best?" I asked the old woman.

"I liked them all. Oh, it was all interesting."

"Really? You had no favorites?"

"No, hardly ever. Even with people, I didn't play favorites."

Something in her attitude struck me as terribly wise and healthy. Too bad she was not a blood relative, and through in-laws our relationship was extremely distant. On the other hand, here she was, an immigrant before World War I, like my grandfather and my grandmother's family, and her life was parallel to a large extent to theirs, except that she had never bothered with Yugoslavia. What struck me about these lives was the absence of men. Most of them had died early because of terrible working conditions in the factories and because of unhealthy lifestyles. This was, in some way, a matrilineal society. My quest for roots here was matrilineal.

After parting from the wise women, we drove to the cemetery. Calvary is huge, with rolling hills and many lots. It took us quite a while to find section *110*, and then the lot—the lots weren't marked. Most of the tombstones were level with the ground and kept up pretty well. It took us half an hour to find her grave. The stone was pretty clean, thanks to Babe. The wind was blowing. My son shivered and stood on the stone. I told him, "You can't stand on the stone."

"Why?" He asked.

"It's not respectful."

"Why?"

"I don't know. Who knows, maybe your great-grandmother would like it, that you are here, standing above her. OK, stand there if you like."

Jeanette took pictures. I planned to send them to my mother, who was eighty-one and ill in Croatia, but it occurred to me that she might not like to see that eighty-one was the biological limit, so far, for women in her lineage. Maybe I would not send her the pictures. Should she die without seeing her mother's and grandmother's graves?

We took a walk to the other section, where Mary's mother was. That one was next to a large maple. I was surprised to see that her first name totally anglicized into Catherine; I had expected her to be Katarina. My daughter danced at her grave, and said, "ABC. Daddy, there's alphabet soup down here!" And she sang, "Now I sing my ABC." We all laughed. Eva had found a good use for tombstones. Later, we will of course revisit, and then, I suspect, Eva will not sing, and as the years go by, the stones would strike a sadder note in her.

EPILOGUE

MY SON'S VIEWS

Until getting on the CN Tower in Toronto and walking on the thick glass floor, which gave him an illusion of walking on air 1500 feet above the ground, a thrill of peril, my son's favorite buildings were the World Trade Center Towers. Joey found it scary to be sitting perched in the glass tower, and he did not want to be pushed, as though he could fall through the glass. But he liked that fear, and seeing helicopters and airplanes fly below us made him laugh.

We walked up on the top in the heavy wind, looked at the Statue of Liberty and Ellis Island. I told Joey how his great-grandfather had gone through that station on false papers to get into the United States. That did not make an impression on him.. To Joey, the story didn't mean anything. Borders, papers, what was all that compared with the grand vision we were having?

He recognized the Empire State Building and the Chrysler Building. We had gone as high as we could on the Chrysler Building, but the top was private space. Those elevators, wood paneled, were beautiful, as was everything about the building, from far, near, and inside, which could not be said about the Twin Towers. Still, the magnetism of gleaming metal surpassed everything in the city for him, and I must admit, for me. When I came to the States for a visit, at the age of eighteen, I had a picture taken with the towers, and my head only, so as much as possible of the building could fit. The kind passerby who took my picture understood what I wanted, and he kneeled on the pavement to look up and to get nearly the whole building with my beheaded version.

After enjoying the sinking sensation in the swift elevator ride, we walked around the towers, and my brother and I marveled at the sheer size. When these buildings become too old and decrepit, how will people take them down? Ivo and I pondered that. Should they use helicopters, starting from the top? They couldn't just implode the buildings, could they? Maybe it would take as much work to take them apart, as it did to put them together. Did the architects think of that when they designed the monsters?

We went to the Border's Bookstore, which was in the towers' underground complex and would later be destroyed as well. We walked into the bookstore to get a few books, including *Skyscrapers*, an elongated book, mimicking a profile of one of WTC buildings. Joey was surprised that there were buildings taller than World Trade Center, in Kuala Lumpur, the Patronias Towers. Joey learned the top ten buildings, with their sizes in feet and meters. For a whole year after the tour of the tall buildings in New York, my son made many drawings of the twin towers, the Empire State Building, and the Chrysler Building. He loved New York. At his preschool in Cincinnati, Ohio, where we lived at the time, when people asked him where he was from, he said, "I am part North Dakota, part Croatia, and part New York". He was most proud of the New York part.

And now, four years later, when he is eight, I have a fellowship to live in New York City as a writing fellow of the New York Public Library. I thought my family would join me in the city, and instead of going to a regular school, Joey would be home schooled, or rather, city-schooled. By seeing all the aspects of the city, and by getting top-level cello lessons, he would learn more in eight months than by sitting somewhere indoors, exposed to the terrorism of elementary school discipline.

I planned that we would start with World Trade Center. Well, the first day of my fellowship was September 10, 2001, and my family wanted to finish up with music lessons and various other projects in Zagreb,, so they changed the original plan and did not come to New York City with me. If they had, we might have, in a jet-lagged state, gotten up early the following day and been up there before nine a.m. on the 11th.

But on the eleventh, I was at the library, and upon hearing what had happened and running out into the street to gaze at the growing cloud, I called home. I thought Joey would be devastated to hear what had happened, he would cry, perhaps, the way he did when his pet turtle died, squashed by a rock. But, he did not cry. He said, "Yes, Dad, I know everything. I have seen the best details and what I haven't seen, Mom has told me. OK. Bye!"

He sounded thrilled, positively excited. I suppose he was excited by tall buildings because they were such a spectacle, and the destruction was an even greater spectacle, so how could I blame him to be swept by the fascination rather than sorrow?

I still don't know whether he is sad about it. I will ask him next time I talk to him. Maybe a turtle has a soul, and the building, no matter how big and fascinating, doesn't, although there are a multitude of souls hovering above Ground Zero. I am writing this at JFK Airport, about to fly on American Airlines to Zagreb, where my wife and two kids had remained, partly because of the World Trade Center disaster, partly because after staying there for a whole semester, they wanted to finish up their school year.

I will ask him whether he misses the towers, whether he wants to play the cello for them, the way people played for Sarajevo. I think he should. He should sit in that pit and play Bach, for the towers, for me, for us. It would be a beautiful sight, the little boy with long blond hair, who looks like a small replica of Kinski, playing mysterious harmonies on that sad instrument.

The Author

Josip Novakovich immigrated from Croatia to the United States at the age of twenty. He studied medicine in Novi Sad, Yugoslavia, theology at Yale University, and literature at the University of Texas at Austin. He has taught at Bard College, Moorhead State University, Antioch University in Los Angeles, and the University of Cincinnati. He currently teaches on the main campus of Penn State University in College Park, Pennsylvania.

His publications include three collections of stories, *Apricots from Chernobyl* (*1995*), *Yolk* (*1995*), and *Salvation and Other Disasters* (*1998*), which won an American Book Award from the Before Columbus Foundation, a Whiting Award, and was a *New York Times* Notable Book of the Year. He has also written two books on the art of writing and co-edited, with Robert Shapard, *Stories in the Stepmother Tongue* (White Pine Press, 2000), a book of stories written in English by immigrant writers in the United States.

His work has been supported by the John Simon Guggenheim Memorial Fellowship Foundation and the National Endowment for the Arts, and by the New York Public Library's Dorothy and Lewis B. Cullman Center for Scholars and Writers. *Kirkus* has named him one of the best story writers of the past decade and *Utne Reader* included him on the list of ten writers who are changing the way we look at the world.

THE TERRA INCOGNITA SERIES:
WRITING FROM CENTRAL EUROPE

Series Editor: Aleš Debeljak

Volume 6
Perched on Nothing's Branch
Poems by Attila Jozsef
Edited by Peter Hargitai
80 pages $14.00

Volume 5
The City and the Child
Poems by Aleš Debeljak
96 pages $14.00

Volume 4
Afterwards: Slovenian Writing 1945-1995
Edited by Andrew Zawacki
250 pages $17.00

Volume 3
Heart of Darkness
Poems by Ferida Durakovic
112 pages $14.00

Volume 2
The Road to Albasan
An Essay by Edmund Keeley
116 pages $14.00

Volume 1
The Four Questions of Melancholy
New and Selected Poems of Tomaž Šalamun
Edited by Christopher Merrill
266 pages $17.00